Presentation Parlour

The Publishers gratefully acknowledge the support of

The Arts Council / An Chomhairle Ealaíon.

Presentation Parlour

Kate O'Brien

POOLBEG

First published by William Heinemann Ltd in 1963

Published in 1994 by
Poolbeg,
A division of Poolbeg Enterprises Ltd,
Knocksedan House,
123 Baldoyle Industrial Estate,
Dublin 13, Ireland

A catalogue record for this book is available from the British Library.

ISBN 1 85371 243 4

Cover painting *A Convent Garden, Brittany* by William J Leech
Courtesy of the National Gallery of Ireland
Cover design by Poolbeg Group Services
Set by Poolbeg Group Services Ltd in Garamond 11/13
Printed by The Guernsey Press Company Ltd,
Vale, Guernsey, Channel Islands

OTHER BOOKS BY THE SAME AUTHOR

Without my Cloak

The Ante Room

Mary Lavelle

Pray for the 'Wanderer'

The Land of Spices

The Land of Summer

That Lady

The Flower of May

As Music and Splendour

*

Farewell Spain

*

Contents

FOREWORD

by

Michael O'Toole

Presentation Parlour was the outstanding achievement of Kate O'Brien's Boughton years. It was written during 1962 when she was sixty-four and newly relocated in the Kent village where she was to spend the remaining twelve years of her life.

The "base clouds" of Shakespeare's 34th sonnet from which she had derived the title of her first novel, *Without My Cloak* (1931), were already o'ertaking her on her way. Boughton was to have provided a fresh start after the artistic and financial disaster of Roundstone. Extravagant and overly generous by nature, she had allowed her Connemara establishment to drain her resources until forced by the bank to sell. Her last two novels, *The Flower of May* (1953) and *As Music and Splendour* (1958), while not exactly failures, had fallen short of the critical and financial success to which she had been accustomed. She was, as she used to say herself, going out of fashion. More ominous still, she was unable to make progress with *Constancy* – the novel she would never finish. In *Kate O'Brien: A Literary Portrait* (Colin Smythe, 1987), her biographer Lorna Reynolds tells us that in those years she was sometimes "tormented to a frenzy by the problem of how, as Shelley said, 'inspiration is a fading coal'."

The fifties had not been a good decade for her. The big success of *That Lady* (1946) had boosted her income and enabled her to buy the large house at Roundstone. But it was to keep her away from her craft of novel writing and involve her in theatre and cinema business which, artistically and financially, proved far less rewarding than originally had been assumed. A restless soul even by the standards of the artistic community – Kate O'Brien lived at far more addresses than even James Joyce – she now felt the lack of stimulation provided by the theatre, the concert hall and the company of fellow intellectuals. She started to rely on alcohol as a substitute for these things and this, combined with a dazzling disregard for financial or household management, soon had her in difficulties.

Her will, written in London in 1961, makes sad reading. The bank had taken her house and she had to be bailed out by her sister, Anne O'Mara, who had bought a small house for her use in the village of Boughton, near Canterbury. Her estate comprised only furniture, books and pictures, which were in storage with CIE in Dublin, and in copyright and fluctuant royalties. At sixty-four, with her artistic powers on the wane, she was faced with what must have been a quite frightening prospect for a person of her age – the need to make an entirely fresh start in life.

In *Presentation Parlour* Kate O'Brien returned to the world of her childhood and early life, seeking there not only the makings of a book but also rest and refreshment. The theme of family had always been one of her strong points. Now in the greater awareness of her own frailty and mortality, she evokes the five aunts who had each – because of the early death of her mother – played an important role in her upbringing. She parades each of these aunts through her Presentation parlour – the parlour of the Presentation Convent in Sexton Street, Limerick, where two of these aunts were nuns and where the O'Briens held many family gatherings. She examines "their outward similarities of tradition, education and faith...their agreement in bigotry, prudence and innocence...their shared loves and anxieties and their half-concealed antipathies."

At the end she asks them to forgive her "impertinent affection" and "vulgar probing". Kate O'Brien believed in what Seán O'Faoláin described as "that impenetrable wall of identity that segregates every human being in a private world of self." In *My Ireland*, the other book of this bleak period, she says: "It is pleasing to consider the uniqueness of possession each one of us has in life. We carry little baggage of any importance for the single journey; but we do go it alone, and no customs officer or shadowy boatman, not the 'fell sergeant' himself, can force us to declare anything. We each take a passage which no other takes, even though over the years and through what for convenience we like to call the same landscape."

Like so many of the characters in her fiction, these aunts were of Catholic families, peasant in origin, which had proved strong enough to be able to survive penal laws, famines, emigration and drag themselves through innumerable obstacles to emerge as pillars of a new Catholic mercantile class. Two of the five had entered the religious life; the others married into families of their own class, and all three of these lived to endure change and a reduction in their fortunes and status.

Presentation Parlour is, first and foremost, a delightful and perceptive memoir of Catholic middle-class life in Ireland during the first two decades of the twentieth century. On that basis alone, it can be savoured and enjoyed by a wide audience.

To the student of Kate O'Brien's fiction – a seemingly ever increasing band – it has many additional attractions. Firstly, it demonstrates her great sense of family. Benedict Kiely's claim that "no Irish novelist has understood so well as Miss O'Brien the meaning of a prosperous house, a solid middle class family, a town not tumultuous enough to be a city yet escaping small-town stagnancy" is fully vindicated here. This sense of position sometimes makes her uncomfortable, even causes slight embarrassment. Even though he was only a couple of generations away from the mud cabin himself, her father, Tom O'Brien, wouldn't allow his children to attend Midnight Mass in St John's Cathedral on Christmas Eve because the "riff-raff of the town was loose at that hour...and he would not have his children meet it." He should not, she added, be judged un-Christian for this. "He was only a clean-habited and affectionate man who wanted to keep us in good health and as long as possible unaware of violence and uproar in life."

Kate O'Brien's understanding of Irish convent life was also unrivalled among writers. Her involvement with nuns and convents lasted throughout the whole of her young life until her early twenties when she gave up teaching. It started even before she could remember, with her father taking his young family on the short drive down Mulgrave Street to the convent of the Presentation where his sisters-in-law, Mary and Fan Thornhill (Mother Margaret Mary and Sister Clare), lived behind the walls. It continued from the age of six to eighteen as a boarder with the Faithful Companions of Jesus at Laurel Hill, then known in Limerick as "the French convent", and continued throughout her academic career in UCD as a resident of Loreto Hall.

Kate O'Brien was the youngest ever boarder at Laurel Hill – she was so tiny that a special chair had to be made for her. The opening chapter of *The Land of Spices* (1941) depicts the reception of three novices in the convent chapel of the Compagnie de la Sainte Famille, watched by "the little new girl, six years old and small for her age...crouched down on her haunches and leaning out over the lower rung of her pew...and there was an expression of busy attention on her face...." The F.C.Js were to become the model for the Compagnie de la Sainte Famille.

The institute to which her two aunts were attracted was a different proposition altogether. Founded in Cork in 1776, it was the first of many such Irish institutes, and its foundress, Nano Nagle, insisted that it should concern itself only with the education and care of the poor. The rule was harsh and, until after Vatican II, the nuns were strictly enclosed. Aunt Mary, much as she was admired by her niece for her strong will and administrative abilities, is nevertheless classified by her as being "among the tiresome and self-centred saints".

This was because of one single and fascinating act of self-mortification which repulsed Kate O'Brien. It has been assumed that Mary, prior to entering the convent, would stand bridesmaid at the communion rails with her adoring younger sister, Katty, who had become engaged to Tom O'Brien of Limerick. In later life Tom O'Brien used to tell of Mary's visits to Limerick during the late summer of 1866 when she came to the city to interview her Reverend Mother and to buy her convent trousseau. "She seems to have made her trip unaccompanied, and father took charge of her in his native city. His engagement to a beautiful girl from the hinterland of East Limerick had been announced: and here he was now, dashing about in his high gig, very gay with a beautiful coppery-haired young woman who was presented, when absolutely necessary, to this or that one as 'Miss Thornhill of Kilfinane'."

Then, a few weeks before the nuptials, came Mary's sudden and – to her family – devastating act of mortification. She decided to enter the convent before, rather than after, the wedding and, after a sharp farewell, fled to the cold silent convent of the Presentation.

To the future novelist whose main theme was to be the consequences of the pursuit of love and freedom by intelligent women, this jot of family history must have been particularly fascinating. But it offended against human generosity – and in Kate O'Brien's catechism that was a serious sin. Interestingly, she doesn't even hint at what has to be another possible scenario for Aunt Mary's sudden flight: the possibility that on those trips to Limerick, she felt attracted to her future brother-in-law or, indeed, he to her.

The Presentation parlour in Sexton Street, Limerick was Kate O'Brien's first theatre of sensibilities. Some of what the child saw and heard here would find its way into her fiction, as well as providing the focus for this most delightful memoir which bears its name.

INTRODUCTION

I had five aunts. So had my brothers and sisters, the same five in name and place. But my five aunts are not theirs any more than theirs are mine. All nine of us had each his own five aunts, in as much or as little as we possessed, observed or remembered them. Were there then forty-five aunts? Maybe. But they lived, conventionally and unassumingly, behind five names and five faces.

On the one hand, there were Mother's three sisters – Aunt Mary, Aunt Fan and Aunt Annie, all younger than Mother. On the other, there was Father's only sister whose name was Anne, but who was known to us by her married surname as Aunt Hickey. She was twenty years older than Father. And there was the wife of Father's quite old brother, Uncle Mick. Her name was also Anne, so she was called Auntie Mick – a kind of pet name which did not become her at all.

These aunts with, in a few cases, accompanying uncles made a constant and lively background to our youth – as aunts and uncles do. But as our mother died when all nine of us were very young – running from fifteen years to nine months – our father, and we with him, became more than is usual dependent upon the five – for authority, fun, advice or affection. And we would have been a lost and queer bundle of orphans without them. Anyway, they were there.

They created impressions. They made from five to forty-five different sorts of dents in the surface of family life. They were, in their contrasted natures, all as emotional as we were – some of them were as distressible. They were an anxious lot on the whole, I think; and they took us very seriously. Poor Katty's children. They took us on, to help Tom – our father, and they found or decided – found, I think they would insist, that they loved us. We found in our turn that we loved some of them. And one of us thinks that perhaps through a long labyrinth of remembrance, and family feeling and plain curiosity, she has arrived at loving them – in an elderly fashion. Perhaps somewhat in the way in which Auntie Mick, she flatters herself, loved her.

Love aside – and who is to define it in relation to the long-dead, the memory-and-wish-invented ? – I have reflected sometimes in my later years on the personalities and lives of these aunts. It interests me to observe that whereas they all came out of the same mould – their fathers having been hard-beaten peasants of the desperate 'forties who had survived to reach the refuge of a town, then courageously to earn their way on to the foothills of the middle-class, they, the daughters, having received only such minimum convent education as could not now be called education, and being all five steeped, but steeped, in Roman Catholicism, of which the conventions and period-bigotries were as unquestionable to them as the rules – were indeed one and the same thing, for my aunts were not theologians – as I began to say, it interests me to recall that they were individuals, to a woman. They were personalities – each with emphasis, even on occasion with clangor and commotion. Sisters-in-law they might be, with interests the same and entangled; and sisters emotionally, even hysterically attached; five of them, reading the same few books, attending similar missions, holding more or less the same political views, all agreed that a certain few things and ideas and ways of life were right, and that a thousand others, not to be mentioned if possible, were totally wrong and abominable – yet these five were separated and different from each other in all that gave them identification of soul as ash tree is from birch, or blue eye from brown.

My recollections are not pure. Time and myself have worked upon my aunts for me, and the portraits I have sketched are perhaps not portraits even in the freest, most expressionist sense, for anyone but me. And even for me, they are not representational or within sight of being photographic. The time is too long; I peer through half-shut eyes from very far away, and the knowingness of adult life cannot help but throw in accents and shadows which the child who knew these women could not have perceived. I must suppose.

Santayana, in his memoirs, ponders the relationship between what the child saw and what he, the man, remembers – and in one place says: "From that coachman's box my young mind saw nothing but the aesthetics of mechanism; yet my unconscious psyche kept a better watch, and I can now evoke images of impressions that meant nothing to me then but that had subtler significance." I would say something similar of how my own long-ago seeing relates to my recalling of what I saw. And I think that my unconscious psyche was an active sprite.

Nevertheless, these portrait sketches, done *con amore* and to refresh and amuse myself, are the unaided work of an elderly woman. I have been earnest to avoid picturesque foreground presentation of that "touching small figure" which most "I" narrators of family chronicles and humours become. I have had to intervene in my youthful guise more often than I find satisfactory, because these women existed for me and gave me my long memories of them simply as my aunts and through their relationship with me. But my attempt now, as a kind of response to all they gave and tried to give – some of them anyway – to the person they saw in me, is to try to re-create them free and in themselves – to try to detach them, if I possibly can, from the states of emotion, fuss, exasperation and temerity in which their concern for us obscured, or half-distorted them.

I have a nephew who when he was a child and schoolboy had, all to himself, seven *bona fide* aunts. Their number has thinned by now. He is an only child and when he first went to boarding-school he found the ways and ideas of boys in herds somewhat surprising. When his mother visited him early in his first term he said this:

"The boys here are often very peculiar, Mamma. Last night a lot of us were talking, and they all kept making fun of their aunts and people! They said they hated their aunts!"

"And what did you say?"

"Oh, I said that I couldn't agree with them at all! I told them that I love my aunts!"

AUNT ANNIE

"Don't tell me you didn't get a telegram?"

"We did not, Annie."

"Well, wait till I catch Willy! And he didn't telephone?"

"If he had you'd have been met at the station, as well you know."

And so the fun was on. She had arrived, as usual, in the afternoon of St Stephen's Day, with her two little daughters. The jarvey man jangled off, and she was here, in the hall, pretty and welcome. And the fun was already peculiar to her direction, in that everyone knew the talk of telegram and telephone to be nonsense, yet there was just a glimmer of question left – so innocent were her eyes.

Where I first pick her up, simply as the person I knew, is here in one or other of these arrivals to stay with us for part of the Christmas holidays. She nearly always did this in our youth, and I cannot be sure of when I began to hear the above annual opening gambit – but perhaps her elder daughter standing at her side was about eight. If so, I was ten. Had she not come on those Stephen's Days the holidays would have been dimmed and reduced. I think that would have been true for most of us. At this time a matron, a grown-up – I suppose she was in her early thirties –

she was, until you looked at her, of conventional middle-class appearance. She was of medium height and not fat, though her figure was not good; old photographs showed that as a girl, at the turn of the century, she was graceful in the severe boned and pleated dresses of the period. Her brown-gold hair was still very pretty at this time, in spite of her industry with curling tongs; her shoulders, neck, head and face had the formal beauty of all the Thornhills, her father, her three sisters and her brother; and her eyes, like theirs, were very blue. But they were small eyes, less deeply placed than those of her relations, and they were outward-looking and very bright. She was the youngest of four beautiful sisters, but there was perhaps that in her temperament that resisted the exigencies of beauty, for, without throwing it quite away, she seemed to turn it into prettiness. Pretty she was; and I think that when she was a girl the word "lovely" would have suggested her more nearly than "beautiful". Her clothes were probably very ordinary, but I remember that she sometimes wore colours that surprised, and were fortunate; she had a silk dress of tobacco brown – I cannot remember when – and it was perfect. She had some brown furs too in which she looked warm and merry.

She was the wife of a grocer and wine-merchant in Fermoy, a very pretty garrison town in County Cork. Her husband was her age, or perhaps a little younger; but if the latter, she would never have admitted it. Uncle Willie was small and blue-eyed, a boyish, tender-hearted man with a great love of teasing and joking; he was a man for innovations and new ideas, and from his far-out fringe on a bank of the Blackwater river he kept his eye cocked on modern progress. He had a telephone in his house immemorially, and also a most amusing blower-contraption from house to shop. He must have been easily the first shopkeeper in Fermoy to install electric light; and one of the first objects that I remember clearly, outstanding on a little table and not like other pieces of furniture at all, is his phonograph, loudly singing "Down By The Old Bull And Bush". He loved to talk and read about motor-cars, and had he lived a little longer he would have soon climbed up behind a steering wheel, in goggles and dustcoat. He had cameras on tripods, with black cloths and a dark room. He was also enthusiastic and enterprising in his inherited shop. He was the third MacCarthy in direct line to own it, and it was a shop with character; its façade, like that of the house above it, was unpretentious, in 1840 Irish small-town manner, and the interior retained the original fittings of brass and mahogany, as well as large dark japanned containers – for rice? for spices? – which were decorated with fading bands of gold leaf and dark red, and had gold leaf hieroglyphics on their rounded fronts. The electric light was fitted into the brass gasoliers that moved up and down.

From this shop his father had sent Uncle Willie, as a young apprentice, to Mincing Lane in London, to learn about tea in a famous importing house. And he did learn how and where to buy tea, and how to taste and blend it. He practised tea-tasting with pride and gravity, and we loved to be allowed to watch him at it. I believe that his shop had always been known in County Cork for the fine sorts of tea it sold; also for its wines. These were profitable wares to have to sell in a garrison town and in hunting country, so when Uncle Willie went courting, about 1897, he must have been a good and attractive match, for a country girl of his own class.

I would not put it past the particular country girl he

got to have thought herself a cut or two above him – which would have been utter nonsense. But utter nonsense was Aunt Annie's strength and shield throughout her life. She was made to live with it; and alas, there is no place where one can do that. Sadness, sometimes called reality, keeps breaking in. Nevertheless, in childhood and youth mirages and illusions can crowd the sky; and Aunt Annie was young for a long time.

She began to be young in babyhood, in Kilfinane. For one thing, she *was* the youngest person always among the family and friends. Actually how much younger she was than her three sisters and her only brother I do not know. She and Aunt Fan used to quarrel sharply about ages, in their middle age. In the convent parlour.

Aunt Fan was a nun, and she was the nearest in age to Aunt Annie of the three older sisters – with their brother Pat between them. Aunt Annie was not at all afraid of Fan. She was somewhat in awe of Aunt Mary, another nun; but Fan and she met on ground they knew, and in disagreement they scuffled it up. Their well-featured faces grew tight when they annoyed each other; and their blue eyes – Fan's the more beautiful – filled with tears. But not tears of yielding or compassion; tears rather of nervous excitation, those tears of fretful irritability of which all descendants of the Thornhill name shed too many, in too many incongruous circumstances.

Fan's ruling about Annie's age, whatever it was, was likely to have been exact. Anyway, Mother was twenty-two in 1886, when she married and left Kilfinane, and I assume Aunt Annie to have been at least twelve or thirteen in that year. But she would never tolerate that a date be fixed for her. She had always been the youngest person she knew or could recall in Kilfinane.

This high-perched village which clings to the top of Ardpatrick is a bleak-seeming place, its only beauty that of situation; westward and south it looks down across the fertile plains of Limerick and north Cork; and south-east it is shouldered by the Knockmealdown mountains, which separate it from the Blackwater Valley. Its two or three streets curve up to meet in a crooked square, beside a big, plain Catholic church. Though fairly large, openly built with solid early nineteenth-century houses and having a well-aired, sober look, Kilfinane has never been prosperous or remarkable. It has none of those sad beautiful evidences of history in which Kilmallock, at its feet, is so tragically rich. But in common with the villages about it, indeed with all poor and rural places of Ireland, it suffered a terrible nineteenth century. And from the 1840s, through the Potato Blight, the Famine, the emigrant trail to the coffin ships at Queenstown, on through the pitiless 'fifties of starvation, eviction and hatred, the agitations and despairs of Fenians and Ribbonmen, to the wild hopes of the Land Wars and the Land League, the flame of courage lighted by Davitt and Parnell – in those any child growing up in a poor or country place, on the land or in a little town, would be aware by more than hearsay of fear and misery and of the savageries of social injustice.

In the 1650s, a soldier of Cromwell's army named Thornhill, having fought at the sieges of Limerick and Clonmel, was garrisoned awhile at Kilmallock, and at the allocation of the lands of the conquered decided to take his share and settle down on the western face of Ardpatrick. He married a girl of the neighbourhood, and almost certainly, if to his surprise, became a Papist. Or if he did not, his children, without doubt, were Papists to a man. And three hundred years later to the very decade, my grandfather, Patrick Thornhill, then only a boy, was having to fight with guile and energy – in common with uncles, brothers, cousins – to hold on to the same lands which the original conqueror had given to their Plantation ancestor.

By the nineteenth century these lands had long ceased, of course, to belong to the Thornhills in the plain sense in which they had been the property of the first Thornhill. The Penal Laws had rapidly seen to that, since all Thornhills, save the first, were Papists, and so automatically reduced to as near serf status as was possible on paper and before the existent law. But in spirit and character they never were serfs at all. That might be guessed from one quick look at Grandfather Thornhill. But the proof of it is that throughout the crazily difficult and tragic nineteenth century, the Thornhills kept on farming and raising good cattle stock with intelligence and success; so that they were able to hold to their lands, meet the fantastic extortions of agent and absentee landlord, keep the trust and respect of their own class and kind, and put money in the bank. To have done all of those things at one and the same time was to be at once spirited, quick-witted and honourable.

When I knew Grandfather Thornhill – briefly, at the beginning of this century – he looked to be all of those things. I know that, because as I write these words I can see him as clearly as I did when he used to dash into our nursery, with Mother laughing at his side. If Mother was with him and well and laughing, that means that I can only have been about three – and Grandfather would have been, I guess, seventy. And two gayer or more distinguished-looking people you could not wish to see. The clarity with which I see them now reminds me, with Santayana, that my "unconscious psyche" kept better watch than I. For in fact those hilarious entrances of Grandfather into our peace did not please me. I knew – and it always happened – that I would be snatched from the quiet perch I occupied, and slung up and down between the ceiling and his watch-chain while he sang, with sickening gaiety:

"Dance her up and up, and
Dance her up on high –
Dance her up and up –
And she'll come down bye – and – bye!
She's the flower of the flock..." etc.

I hated that. I was sure that one day in excess of vitality he would dash me against the ceiling; also I found the whole outburst foolish. All that interested me in it was the curious gold ornament that hung from his watch-chain; but speed of passage up and down from it made examination impossible.

I disliked that gay, graceful man whom Mother seemed to enjoy so much. But I remember that he was slim – not thin, like an old man, but slim like a young one, that he wore grey cut-away tweeds, that his eyes were blazing blue, and that his hair waved back over his ears, rather wet, like the hair of a setter dog.

Now I wonder at those warm high spirits. For many disappointments and sorrows lay behind them – and at that time he must have been facing agony. Mother, in her thirty-seventh year, was beginning to die; and Grandfather would have known that. And she was not only his first-born, but – as everyone acknowledged – his idea of all that was beautiful, and the very core of his heart.

So a cross little child being annoyed by the gaiety of a handsome old man does not know everything, psyche or no psyche.

This deviation into my own time seems to me

helpful in trying to catch the Thornhill quality. Intellectually, cerebrally, I do not think that they were endowed. Granted that they received no education to prove or disprove this, granted even that Mother and Aunt Mary both had, for the ordinary needs of life, what we call brains – still I think that amongst them no intellectualism was lost; because it never is lost; it is self-educating, and it demonstrates itself in any life where it is – however crudely. But intelligence they had – scattered and uncertain. Comic and inverted sometimes; sometimes absent, or perverse. Often too much ridden by sensibility, to which indeed they were foolish martyrs. Sometimes misled by intuition. But in general the family was possessed, for better and for worse, of a refining and nervous intelligence of the heart. It was of little use to them, because they did not understand it. And they did not understand it because it is exactly a tricky, irritable, sweet and morbid kind of intelligence which cannot be understood, from within or without. None of us can define it. All we can do is recognise it. It makes around it a kind of muffled, innocent romanticism; it makes for quarrels, touchiness, generosity – and it tends always to set affection in authority over intelligence, over the basic, troublesome thing, *intelligence* of the heart. Affection is not the captain in the human condition, so confused, that I am seeking to expose. But it is a bully, a dominant – and creates pain and question which the analytic intellect could assault and in so doing help, but against which mere instinctive intelligence – however in doubt – is helpless.

Intuitional intelligence at its best is a poor weapon. It is a sword that bends. Against the shields and blunt daggers of reason it is useless – though against them it does not break. Rather it springs back, boomerang fashion, and can wound the hand that holds it. And at its worst, as often it has to be, it can hardly be called intelligence of any kind, but only intuition off-beam. Then it is dangerous.

Grandfather Thornhill married – I surmise about 1862 – a handsome young lady, well endowed, from Cork. Of the Sheedy family. She was out of the rich merchant class, and she brought good looks and exact bourgeois standards to the house over the shop in the main street of Kilfinane. (Grandfather, for some reason which must have had to do with the very tricky tenure troubles of the time, never lived on any of his two or three rich farms, but kept a general shop and his family house in the centre of Kilfinane.) I say she brought good looks, but they were of the Roman-emperor kind that blunted here and there in descent the sharp, clean-edged beauty of Grandfather's line; and I think that certain descendants, Aunt Fan for one and I for another, can blame Grandmother Thornhill in some measure for our decline from good looks into a too heavy handsomeness. I remember being lifted up once to kiss her good night – beautifully smocked nightgown and white hair in faultless plaits – a very handsome white face. I was about seven then, and Mother was long dead. I suppose I resented the existence of her old mother. But anyway, that was the only occasion of meeting my grandmother that I remember – and I did not like her. I saw that she was handsome, large and calm. My psyche could not jump forward to tell me that what I shrank from in that comfortably settled bed was a pre-view of my elderly self.

These then were the parents and this the home and playground of Aunt Annie and her sisters: the hilly streets of a lonely little town, and the fields below the graveyard on Ardpatrick.

She went to the village school, and to no other. So

did Mother; when the time had come for *her* to be "finished" at a convent boarding-school, she had begged off, to Grandfather's great delight, and had taken private lessons, in pianoforte, embroidery and so on, from some nice local old maids. Mary and Fan had however been compelled to a couple of years each at an Ursuline convent. But when it came to Annie her father – no doubt depressed by the vocations for the religious life with which the "finished" pair came home – let her off; and she, like Mother, ran frivolously about the village, with her portfolio and her needlework, between the gentle parlours of Miss Roche and Miss Lee. I think Grandfather need hardly have worried about losing the last of his four beauties to cloister vows; for Annie would as likely have become a nun as decide to take up the study of Greek. But her skimpy education served. She wrote clear and fluent letters that brought her voice and her laugh with them; she never used a word which she did not understand; her punctuation and spelling were not to be faulted, and her handwriting to the end of her life was shapely, confident and legible. And she was critical of letters she received. Later in years, when as a widow she was having to try to run her husband's shop, she could get quite crazy fun out of, say, "Yours to hand and contents noted". I have seen her sing it, rhyme it and dance it – with the bailiffs practically settling in.

But the little girl skipping to and from school in the early 1880s – (I take her to have been born about 1873, and she has been so long asleep with her secret now that she will not hear my impertinent guess) – had yet some way to go before she would have to spell "bailiff".

Pretty, indeed enchanting as she must have been, lighting the street and the schoolyard as she ran, she still was not the type of "teacher's pet". Ah, naïve would have been the teacher who made a pet of Annie Thornhill! For graceful, friendly and all-things-to-all-men though she seemed – and I have often seen her as near as wink overdo her kindly charm – she was from cradle to grave without respect of persons.

That is a clue to her. She respected her religion indeed; deep, native faith placed it outside of everyday range. But she did not confuse it with its ministers; she could sit giving tea with grave politeness to some bumbling or conceited priest and only if you knew her well would you understand that behind the clear, friendly eyes she was enjoying him with savagery. And her formidable sister Mary, even when a Reverend Mother, could not suppress Annie if she wanted to mock a bishop. And Aunt Mary was seen to laugh at some of those audacities.

She respected the major conventions of society too – and indeed to excess, as did all of her period. But the persons within them – oh, they, were they her own beloved children, were they any of us, dear Katty's children, were they De Valera or Parnell or the Archbishop of Cashel – they were all isolated, ordinary human beings, and at any given moment she might find them exquisitely amusing. And if she did, she was able to convey that amusement. Aunt Annie 'put over' her jokes and humours with more skill and speed, I think, than anyone I have ever known – except Fay Compton. But I shall return to that.

There is no doubt that the child is father to the man, so I have always assumed about Aunt Annie that her sense of fun, her satirical turn, were proportionately as marked in the little girl of the village as they were in the bourgeois matron that I knew.

She was a great messenger, always flying from here to there, on the instruction of her mother, or of Katie

Brown, their servant. This fact about her was caught in a poem by Tom O'Dea:

"And Annie, the babe, was sent out in a shower,
With a three-cornered note, to tell Mrs Power
That Maggie, in pink, was the life of the party..."

That satirical poem by Thomas O'Dea rips open the social scene in Kilfinane in the autumn of 1886.

Katty Thornhill had become engaged to Thomas O'Brien of Limerick. They were to be married before Advent, and her father, not a convivial man, decided that he must give an evening party, to present his future son-in-law to Kilfinane.

This Tom O'Brien was by Kilfinane standards, indeed by any, a man of the world. He was in fact a child of the post-famine evictions, for his father had been turned out of his small holding – near by, in Bruree country – about 1850, and had made his way with wife, young daughter and two sons, and with a few household remnants on an ass-cart, as far as Limerick. Then, middle-aged and ill, he had sought about for a new way of living. He began to buy and sell horses. He had a flair for horses. And in a very short time he made himself an expert on the breeding of blood stock, hunter and harness thoroughbreds. During the first or second year of this new beginning his last child – twenty years younger than his only daughter – was born. By the time this boy Tom was leaving school his father was an admired citizen of Limerick, and was building himself a brick villa to flank the paddock and stables where he had based his business of blood-stock breeding.

He already had a large stud farm, and was buying pure-bred stallions.

The late-born son, Jesuit-schooled in Limerick, and

sent by his father at an early age to learn and make mistakes at Tattersall's and Newmarket, had inherited that father's flair. Between them, young man and old, they grew to be regarded as first authorities in Ireland on thoroughbred horseflesh.

There is a colour-wash photograph of this grandfather, mounted in purple velvet and framed in gilt, in my brother's house in Shropshire. One could lead people to it and say – "Who do you think he was? What kind of person?" They would likely say: "John Stuart Mill." Or, "Is he a Unitarian?" Or, "Any connection of Cardinal Newman?" No one could ever guess from that elegant and emaciated old man that he was an evicted Irish peasant who had avenged himself on England by making a great fortune in selling to her superb hunters and superb blood carriage horses.

His last, so late-born son, was physically unlike him. He was short, stocky, Roman-headed, with thick, close-cut dark hair, bright blue eyes and a clipped moustache. He dressed well, in tweed cutaways; his hands were freckled, expressive and well cared for; everything about him was of good taste and quality, from cigar to boot to handkerchief. He had superb teeth, and all thirty-two of them went down with him into his grave in his sixty-third year. When I, his youngest daughter, knew him best, in my schoolgirl years up to his death in 1916, he looked extraordinarily like Arthur Schnabel of the 1940s.

This wealthy and gay Tom O'Brien, aged thirty-three, and with an experienced eye for women, was the *parti* that Patrick Thornhill had notched down for his darling, his idol. Where he met him, when and why he chose him we do not know. But there is a story that he brought the rich stranger into his house in Kilfinane one day, for entertainment or refreshment of some kind. His eldest daughter absenting herself from the parlour, he sent her a message to descend immediately. She sent back word – probably by the child Annie – that she preferred not to appear. She had fallen downstairs that morning, and was in consequence having to wear a sticking plaster across the bridge of her nose. She begged to be excused.

Her father – always a martinet, I suspect – would not excuse her. And meek as one might not have expected her to be, from other stories – the eldest daughter came to the parlour, and was presented to her future husband.

Well then in October came the need to give the party.

Patrick Thornhill was in high good humour, because his darling had accepted the courtier he had designed for her, and seemed very happy with him. The courtier pleased him too. He was a romantic, a man of imagination. He had bought some historic O'Brien diamonds, from the house of the Earls of Clare, and had had them set in a ring for Katty. He was gay and unexpected – always turning up in his beautiful gigs, or on a thoroughbred mount, with this or that surprise. Not Katty only, but Mary and Fan and Annie were in love with Tom O'Brien. So let them have a splendid party. But the list of the invited must be submitted to the head of the house.

It was – and he passed every name, save O'Dea. He struck his pencil through that word, and said that no O'Dea was coming to the party.

He could have done nothing more awkward.

The Thornhills loved the O'Deas and the O'Deas loved the Thornhills – all except Patrick Thornhill and Thomas O'Dea, the fathers of the two families, who despised each other.

It may not be for nothing that Grandfather bore a Puritan patronymic. When he expressed his dislike of

Thomas O'Dea he never went farther than to say that the man "had something of the gipsy about him". But he said it from time to time, and that was enough.

Whatever about gipsy strain, Tom O'Dea was known to everyone as a real joker of a man – and a good joker. Whether he had a shop or a farm I cannot tell. What he did have was a number of mixed, light talents, a good-humoured wife who enjoyed these, and four children, dark-haired and dark-eyed as himself, who inherited some of the talents. The children, four of them, Mary, Alice, Harry and Bernardine, ran more or less for ages with the Thornhill girls, the last-named Annie's class mate, and the elder girls at the time of the party being at that ripeness of adolescence when the engagements and marriages of other girls are subjects of radiant interest and delight. And Katty Thornhill, grown-up now and beautiful, was with her sisters their great, great friend. Moreover, as all the Thornhills were forever in and out of Mrs O'Dea's house, with their own mother's full approval, it was impossible to consider the O'Deas' absence from the only large party that Patrick Thornhill ever decided to give.

Grandmother tackled her husband with perfect coolness. It was no less than idiotic, she told him, to suggest that the O'Deas were not to come to Katty's party. And she kept on saying so, into his smiling silence. Everyone intervened – all the children, all the more trusted friends; Miss Roche and Miss Lee. The Canon put in a strong word for neighbourliness. Katty herself, the promised bride with the great hoop of diamonds flashing on her unaccustomed hand – and a lovely ring it is too; I have never seen diamonds better set or looking so like tears – Katty, relying on her tremendous power over this wilful man, told him that it would be her last and only request before she left his house, to invite her friends, the O'Deas, to the party.

Extraordinarily, he did not give in.

Then Grandmother said there had better be no party. And Grandfather said: "As you will."

Had I been Grandmother I would have stuck to that, I think. It surely would have been the right thing to do ? But one must suppose that arrangements were forward, and that such a general disappointment was not to be faced. And the light-hearted and well-mannered O'Deas understood the absurd situation, and did not let it cloud their love of the Thornhills.

Still, Grandfather behaved badly that time, and cast a silly shadow on his beloved daughter's last days in his house. And Tom O'Dea, guitar-player, piano-player, singer and rhymer and all-round gay *farceur*, did not let him get altogether away with his pomposity; for, twenty-four hours after the great party, an imaginative description of it, in verse, was travelling about Kilfinane. It was signed, and in the fine O'Dea handwriting, and friends and neighbours were not remiss in showing it to Patrick Thornhill.

It had excellent and cruel lines in it, and a very fine, benevolent passage explaining why it was impossible that O'Deas could attend such a party. From Aunt Annie I often heard especially that passage, with delight. But now I find that it is gone. Only one irrelevant line I remember, descriptive of some important lady's *grande toilette*: "Simple and grand, with a bow on the side of it...."

About the O'Deas: When Harry was seventeen he saw some London touring players in the Opera House in Cork. He want backstage, talked to the manager, and joined them. After a year or two he wrote to his sister Mary, who was bored now in Kilfinane, to come to London; he would undertake to get her on to the stage. With her parents' amused approval, she went.

Harry was by this time stage-managing and playing

small parts in Lily Langtry's company. Mary got into repertory, and they took a flat. And not long behind her sister, Alice O'Dea, came to join them. She also became an actress. Mary, the eldest, did not stay many years on the stage; her health was not good. But the other two, doing quite well in their profession, were able to support her, and she kept house for them until her death.

None of the three lived to be very old. I met Harry only once, when I was a small child and he came to Limerick to see his youngest sister. I remember that he was a pleasant and unusual kind of man, who made good jokes. He was very dressy, and had extremely sad, burning dark eyes, in an ugly, sad face. Alice I knew in London in the late 'twenties of our century, when she was an established character actress. Harry was dead by then. She was large and tall, with a fine and subtle voice, a shade too deep for general purposes. She may be remembered by elderly playgoers for a success she had in the 'twenties, in a farce starring Sybil Thorndike, called *Advertising April*. Alice made a brief appearance in the second act as a Royal Personage, visiting a film studio. She was built to play the part, knew how to play it – and had a triumph. However, she also had the agony of having to play it once with Queen Mary in the Royal Box.

The fourth O'Dea, Bernardine – Aunt Annie's class mate – lonely, temperamental, inclined to music – became a nun, in the severe, enclosed order of the Presentation, at its Limerick house, where two of the Thornhills, Mary and Fan, had already taken their vows.

These are the four whom Grandfather would not have at his party. The Cromwellian had smelt the "rogues and vagabonds".

In the years after Katty's marriage life's focus turned

westward from Kilfinane's hilly streets to Limerick where she lived, and where also Mary was, pursuing a severe novitiate in the Presentation Convent. First Fan, from her convent school, went on holiday visits, meeting gaiety and the world there, in a small, bright shape. She found herself well pleased with Katty's new status, and in due course infatuated with Katty's firstborn, a child called May. On these visits to Limerick the young girl spent every hour which rule permitted in the convent parlour with her sister Mary. And when she was nineteen, when she had folded her hair into its first chignon, when Katty and Tom were coaxing her to choose a ball dress and venture on grown-up life, she said "NO" – she was going to join Mary. And so she did.

Annie was lonely in Kilfinane as one by one her sisters vanished west, and her only brother went away to school; but it is improbable that she was depressed. Between the novels that she took to reading, never to desist – and the frequent letters from Limerick, her imagination was engaged. And although her father held the reins while she was still taking instructions from Miss Roche and Miss Lee, after Fan's saddening departure to be a nun home discipline weakened. It is possible that Grandmother said that all by herself Annie might get melancholy, and asked Grandfather if he really wanted another nun in the family.

Pious as he was, it is certain that he did not. And he inclined always to think that wherever Katty was was a good place for anyone to be. So Annie, in youth and young womanhood, was allowed much and prolonged visiting – to Boru House in Limerick, and also to her mother's proud and wealthy relatives in Cork. But except for the Opera House, and perhaps sometimes to buy clothes, Annie was not very fond of visiting Cork. Limerick was her idea. And when Mother was a young matron there, Limerick, the Limerick she gathered round her, that flocked to her indeed, was light-hearted and decorative.

I remarked to an English friend lately – we were talking of our parents – that it is curious that no one, but *no* one, of one's adult acquaintance had ever had a plain or a homely sort of mother.

She smiled.

"But my mother *was* beautiful," she said.

And so was mine. By all the standards, all the records and references, this Katty Thornhill, eldest sister of Annie, who came to Limerick, quickly raised a large family, and died untimely, was memorably beautiful. The whole city, to which she was only a nonentity-stranger, acknowledged that, welcomed her for it, and remembered her long because of it. And I, in the few flash-lit memories that I have of her – in all of them she is either smiling or outright laughing – endorse indeed the general legend – for I can see still her radiantly lovely face.

But, for general life, she was better than beautiful. She was outgoing, light and generous of spirit, a hostess, and a spender of herself. She was to have a short and exacting life, with deep shadows on it here and there, and passages of anxious disappointment, for she had married a gay and generous and adoring, but not an easy or a disciplined man. And at the end she was to have much suffering, and there was to be a general despair and woe.

But, clearly she was one who put into life all she had – with grace and power to make her contribution in forms of hospitality and friendliness, and a charm to which all were susceptible.

In her house her young sister Annie was to be "finished" as neither Miss Roche and Miss Lee nor an Ursuline Convent could have finished her; her talent for gaiety was to be educated here, and the house was to give her years of fun – when she was a girl, and afterwards too, when Mother was gone, and we, her nieces and nephews, were her targets and her pleasure.

When she was seventeen she was reading by the drawing-room fire in Boru House when an eccentric-looking priest was shown in. She stood up. He stared past her. He had a very white face, wide green eyes, and a general air of poverty and untidiness.

"Where is Katty?"

"She's out, Father," said Annie.

He said no more, and threw himself into an armchair.

The young girl had never seen him before, and he was unlike any curate or clergyman of her experience. He sat with folded arms and closed eyes.

"She should be home soon," she ventured.

He did not react.

"Would you like tea?"

He did not move or open his eyes.

"Shall I see if Tom is at home?"

No movement. Annie knelt and fussed with the fire.

"Would you like a cigar?" she suggested.

Then she let him have his way, and settled back to her own chair; but she thought it would be impolite to reopen her novel, so she just sat.

Presently Katty swept in, in street clothes; and the eccentric priest, on his feet and laughing, was all alive. He waved towards Annie.

"That's the young sister? She'll do, Katty. She has decisiveness. I saw her face in the exact second when she settled to leave me to my boorishness. And she stuck to her decision. Not usual in your sex."

This priest's name was O'Riordan. He was a cousin of our father, and at this time a curate in a very poor parish. He was an original and something of a saint – the kind who gave everything away – his overcoat, his umbrella, his hat. He never had a watch, and never knew when he stood up from his writing table whether it was day or night – so he had been known to call casually on Tom or Katty at three in the morning. He was a scholar and sociologist, afterwards of some fame. He went on to be rector of the Irish College at Rome, and a prince of the Church. The tales of his eccentricity are many. But perhaps one of the surprising twists in his austere and lonely nature was his devotion to Mother, and his knack of coming alight and gay in her presence.

Aunt Annie never forgave him that first encounter, and said she always found him impossible.

That was not her general experience with men. She found none but that curate impossible – because they always played the game her way; and also in that half of her mind which was not novelettish, she really delighted in bores. But that was an acquired taste. When she was a girl I imagine she must sometimes have been at sea with her sense of the absurd.

From seventeen until she married Annie led a life which must have been for the most part carefree, and to her taste. For a girl of her period and class she had much liberty, plenty of pocket money and pretty clothes. Dutiful periods at home in Kilfinane with her parents were brightly striped by frivolities in Cork, occasional visits to Dublin, to attend a cousin's wedding or such; and long months in Limerick, where real gaieties – boating parties, picnics, charity bazaars and amateur theatricals were always taking place, and where also, apart from the lively pleasure she took in Katty's first babies, she was in the same place where her three sisters were. And that was, one thinks looking back, more than a happiness for those four

Thornhills. It was a need in them to be within reach of one another, a compulsion perhaps stronger than any – though unrecognised.

Annie's memories of the social to-and-fro of that period took on in narration something of the mischievous glamour of one of her favourite novelists, a writer called Mabel Barnes-Grundy. This lady wrote at some time a tomboy romance called *Molly Bawn*, the text of which, in the days when I knew her, was never far from Aunt Annie's reach. It was about a ravishing Irish creature capering round among lords in English country houses – and never coming to a pin's harm. A few tears here and there, a number of situations of absurdity, some good jokes – and perfect love. As far as I remember, a very naïve and merry taming of a shrew.

Give my aunt her due, she never in her personal reminiscences painted herself as the sure-fire enchantress that her idolised *Molly Bawn* was; but the happy past, for others besides herself, took on the sweet and foolish glow that she appreciated in her novel-reading.

In Mother's first years in Limerick she and Father drew round them, or were members of, quite a "set" of young people, bachelors, married pairs and some young ladies – Egans, O'Maras, Ebrills, Gaffneys, Bourkes, names still about, but the generation, all of it, long asleep – who seem to have been lively, extravagant, fond of fun, and fond of Mother. And Mother's young sister was a very pretty foil – and oddly amusing.

She, Annie, found this set and their capers and ins-and-outs sufficiently like the creatures of printed romance. And if close-up not flawless copies – then there was the joke of that default, which she must early have begun to see and reckon with. And always she could back away to the focus that pleased her. She never was, I think, one for sustained close-up.

Besides these indigenous characters, there were Tom's customers from England, some of whom came to stay sometimes, either at his house, or at his elder brother's – to choose hunters, to hack about, to look for perfect carriage pairs. Exotics, they entertained young Annie very much; she trained her eye on them, and played her cards gaily. And they may occasionally have overcalled their hands, against the local conventions. To change the metaphor, they did not always know the Irish Ladies' (Catholic) Hunt Rules. And so, politely, sometimes they had to be barred the field. But no harm done – no offence given or taken – and such misunderstandings brought life briefly into the reality of *Molly Bawn*.

Other realities, those of common adult life, were moving up always, of course, behind the happy platform. Bleak bits of scenery, not lighted yet, but in position. Katty, for instance, whatever her beauty and self-control suggested, was learning to live with anxiety and disappointment; with an excess too of selfish love. At home in Kilfinane the quiet parents were watching the indolent and self-indulgent moral growth as well as the physical fragility of their only son. And Mary and Fan, in their convent, each battling her own way with the hard life she had undertaken, saw shadows stretching over to them from those, above all from the eldest sister, whom they had not been able to tear out of their hearts.

The years – from 1880 onwards into the 'nineties – were filled with heightened savageries of the Land War. Friends and neighbours, indeed all of Ireland's rural population, were in trouble, in grief, in penury, and decent people were dying as the humiliated paupers that they had never been in life. Economically and politically Ireland was in misery – and the personal tragedy of Parnell flung all across the land an unmanageable, an undiscussable despair. Undiscussable, that is, by young ladies.

That is why I refer here to the public woes of the Land War and of Parnell which were the back-cloth of Aunt Annie's happiest years – because in later life I never heard her mention either; nor of course did I ever hear any other of my aunts speak of Parnell. (Impossible, before the children.) But as I knew how very deeply and angrily Mary and Fan in the convent felt and remembered evictions and land wrongs, often as a girl I wondered how much or little that so near past had meant to Annie. I never heard. But I was to see her cool contempt and honour when the Black-and-Tans came to Ireland.

Parnell, whose disgrace, death and long post-mortem can still fascinate any Irish person, tempts me to deflection now – but the jump would be absurd, into my own girlhood when my father used to talk, sometimes with tears in his eyes, of the lost leader. He had always followed him, in heart and in clear voice; and so brought us all up to admire John Redmond, who had led the minority of faithful in the awful split in that Committee Room of the House of Commons. Father liked to recount some of the bitter witticisms of that occasion – which Auntie Mick did not think fit for young ears. But I – never much interested in political deviations and always concerned as to persons and their private decisions – was strongly swayed towards the rather dull John Redmond, because of that brave hour in Committee Room No. 15. That, however, has nothing to say to Aunt Annie, and I never knew what she thought about Parnell and Mrs O'Shea.

They would not have fitted into her novelistic scheme – even though both were Protestants, which was an enormous help to private arguers, if not at all to politically battling Ireland. Their exposed dilemma was too clear, and offered no soft escapes. They were not young, and their story was not offered in Marie Corelli's prose, but in the law court reporting of *The Times*.

Now the utmost Aunt Annie could take, in her reading, of passion or sin, was what Marie Corelli or Ouida or Hall Caine presented. And I think that she was never quite easy with their emotionalism. She was, although she did not understand this, naturally satirical. I remember once when I was about eighteen and staying in her house, finding her, for lack of a new novel, sloppily ingurgitating an old day-dream – Marie Corelli's *Thelma*. Almost the only *sad* romance that she swallowed whole. I took the book out of her hands and started teasing her about it. Apart from the heroine's icy goings-on, there was a sub-plot in English high society. Lord Somebody's wife was committing adultery. And the lord found out, and I remember reading to Aunt Annie the reproachful address he made to his wife. I remember this much: "Clara, Clara, fallen rose of womanhood..." And I remember how wonderfully Aunt Annie laughed, and began to make a song and a small ballet out of the phrase – that is why I remember it – while I put on a kettle and made tea.

She was very nimble, even in my day, when she had varicose veins and wore elastic bandages. She could skip around, making up steps and tunes to any joke or line that took her. So I remember "Clara, Clara, fallen rose of womanhood..." as this witty-faced spectacled, broken-up widow skipped about her dilapidated little drawing-room and made an absurd song of it. And I can see her beautiful son Bill coming into the room, golden-haired quiet schoolboy – putting down his fishing-rods, raising his brows – "What's this dance?" and joining in with her, delighted: "Clara, Clara, fallen rose of womanhood..." round they went, extemporising wonderfully.

This jump forward into her hard latter years to the time of my real acquaintance with her presents me, head-on, with my long-considered theory about her. I think Aunt Annie might have been a great actress. And I am saying nothing amateurish now. I never saw her stand up in company and give any kind of one-man entertainment; she told me that she never took a part in the amateur theatricals to which Mother's set, the Bourkes, Lloyds, etc., were prone; she liked to paint their faces, she said – and hold the prompt book. We used to force her, when she was in her forties, into our charades – but whatever she was compelled to do in them, or in our absurd game, Statues, she did in violent protest – and always more amusingly than anyone else. She had a thin, pretty singing voice – but would have died rather than stand up by the piano – as too many did – and oblige with a solo. Indeed, for all these parlour sports she liked to have a good position on the side-line. For she enjoyed human folly very much indeed.

No – no amateur. But supposing she had gone through the mill, supposing she had young enough been plunged into professional theatre, she had, I am sure, the root of what that takes. Had she been a Kilfinane child, O'Dea rather than Thornhill – ah but no! Because then she would not have had the Thornhill beauty, which would certainly have been a golden stirrup, a lucky bridle, had she been mounted at all for the theatrical stakes.

I never thought about theatre – of which indeed I then knew nothing – when in my teen-ages and early twenties I was enjoying my aunt's power to entertain.

I knew nothing of timing, of throw-away, or of cut. Neither did Aunt Annie; but I see now that she was a natural mistress of those skills, and so she was a natural non-bore. She never saw herself as being clever or amusing, but once into any funny situation she had no bother with notions of dignity – so she could fool.

And taken unawares she could be athletically funny. One day when she was in her forties my sister Nance and I were enjoying her company in our drawing-room when some young brother nipped in from the study to say that Father M. was in the hall and was desiring to call on Aunt Annie. She listened to the news and then – there was not a second to be lost – I don't know what or who was in her normal path – she cleared the sofa with a kind of vault (I can see her now) and she was barely through the folding doors into the study – was she? – when Father M. was announced and entered the room. Quicker or better farce one could not ask for. Father M., a childhood acquaintance of our acrobatically absconded aunt, was used to a warm welcome wherever the ladies were, and cannot have suspected the wonderful athletic flight from the room which, at the mention of his boring name, we had witnessed. I can only hope that Nance and I kept straight faces and behaved as ladies.

This exploit will rightly suggest that there was nothing of the tragedienne about my aunt. No, it has never been possible for me, looking back, to see her as heavy "lead". Though I have seen her plunged often in common life's grief and woe – sometimes for others, sometimes for her own confusions and mistakes, she never played the heroine. She could cry herself silly, and she could get extremely cross and unreasonable, but she never went upstage.

"Ah, Mother, stop that like a good girl," one or

other of her devoted daughters would say. "Would you like some tea?" And she would respond and smile, and drink several cups of tea with gratitude.

She loved the theatre – but so did everyone in our family, and that had nothing to do with the hidden talent I am talking about. Nor had her craze for the cinema – "The pictures" as we said in 1912 and onwards. Her enjoyment of the pictures was as simple as ours – but it was in her antic and snap references afterwards to what we had seen that she proves herself in my memory a natural comic. I think that it must have been with her, in the Assembly Rooms in Fermoy, that I saw most of Pearl White's serials – certainly *The Perils of Pauline*, or any of the ones I remember. There were more romantic films that Aunt Annie and I adored: *Comin' Thro' The Rye* with Alma Taylor, and *The Bridge-Builder* with Aubrey Smyth – but my chief craze then was for Pearl White, and Aunt Annie, although she was very appreciative of that actress, particularly enjoyed a series called, I think, *The Iron Man*, in which an actor called Craig Kennedy was the star. The iron man itself – a sort of robot – terroriser, though we did not have the word "robot" yet – enchanted Aunt Annie. I did not find him either interesting or funny; she thought him both. And sometimes when we came out of the Assembly Rooms it was difficult to get her to walk home over the bridge in her own manner, so rapturously invaded was she by the whole personality of the automaton she had been watching. But once home there was no holding her. She iron-manned about the place in sheer delight at the foolery. And hours later, when you had managed to get to bed – for she was the most merciless of night-birds – when at last you were just asleep, round your door he would come, very quiet, absolutely ridiculous – Aunt-Annie-Iron-Man.

I can see her now, small, dressing-gowned figure with her hair in curlers, her glasses catching the moonlight and helping her "Act" – rigid, automatic – enjoying herself outright – and knowing that she would force a last laugh out of me. As she did – and as the absurd recollection does now, after fifty years.

I am going to leave her to her midnight follies for a while. I have much more to tell of her – but in relation to her sisters and sisters-in-law; above all, in relation to Fan, her sparring partner.

AUNT FAN

I have sometimes thought it a pity that Fan, who died in 1953 aged eighty-five, did not live to see the pictures of Pope John XXIII, especially some of the smiling, soft ones taken in the strange hour, for him, of his election to the papacy. For in those pictures he seemed to me to be the very image, the twin, of that dear, amusing, and eccentric old nun; and indeed I never see any picture of him without being reminded of Fan.

This proposition, had she been there in her shawls and veils by the parlour window for me to offer it, would at first have made Fan shy, and she would have protested. For to be like His Holiness in anything – Ah, no! But I would point out that, Vicar of Christ indeed, Pope John would be the first to tell her that he was only a man – the son of a working farmer, as she the daughter of another such. And that the accident of resemblance was undeniable. Soon she would put on her gold-rimmed glasses – how much more elegant than all our tortoiseshells! – and smiling, she would set herself to study the picture of the Pontiff. Looking then very brilliantly like him.

And when presently a lay sister came with my luncheon – for when, after long absence, you visited imperious Fan the convent kitchen did you proud –

my aunt, keeping a sharp eye on the service (she was exacting), would suddenly smile and say: "What do you think, Lucy? Miss Kate O'Brien says that I am like His Holiness, if you please!"

Little Sister Lucy would not know what to think, and smiling would bow herself out. But the idea had been accepted; it pleased Fan, and so henceforward it was true. She looked like John XXIII.

Alas, that she missed the pleasure.

But if she looked like the Pope, and in her old age may have had some measure of his benevolence, it is probable that never were two characters less alike.

Fan's name in religion was Sister Clare. When she died she had long celebrated her diamond jubilee as a nun; and was by a considerable length the oldest member of her community. In all those years she had never been offered, or for one moment herself considered, governmental office of any kind. She had never been elected to be Mother Bursar, Mistress of Novices, Mother Assistant, Reverend Mother – or even Mother Sacristan. She had remained for all of sixty-seven years, in one narrow place, in one enclosed group, simply Sister Clare – hypochondriacal, lazy, timid; pious and in an elusive kind of way almost intelligent; escapist and imaginative; earthbound by her affections against which she was helpless – and by them, for the ones she loved, rendered worldly and calculating – in that way in which only nuns, and nuns of a peculiar vintage, can be almost idiotically worldly.

This Presentation Order that she joined – an early nineteenth-century foundation – had a hard rule. Until quite recently, it was absolutely enclosed – meaning that the postulant entered the house outside of which she would never step again, and in whose garden she would be buried; with some measure of the old contemplative rigours and office readings the nuns of Presentation had to combine hard, realistic teaching of the children of the poor. Large crowded schools, great classes of very poor and in Aunt Fan's young days very dirty and wild children, boys and girls, had to be dealt with daily, against a background of prayer, austerity and silence.

The convent in Limerick had a curious charm. It was set down – probably there first – to the north of the railway station, and encircled by small nineteenth-century streets that were orderly and respectable when the convent was young, but have gone down in the world. But the house where the nuns live is a large, late Georgian merchant's-mansion type – not embellished or beautiful, but plain and spacious; it is completely walled-in from the town, and its gardens are long and quiet, and run in three parallel divisions – visitors' garden, cloister garden, and kitchen garden – from the convent proper to the great schools and playgrounds where the nuns work all day.

As child and girl I walked very often, from the Sexton Street gate up the long first garden – the visitors' – to the convent, and then up the steps to the wide Georgian hall door. I liked that walk – even if anxious in case Sister Baptist or Mother Ita might skip out from behind the privet hedge on the left and start gushing at me, or else perhaps at the tricky point where a little gate on the left led into the cloister garden, Sister Benignus might appear – still, it was interesting. The formal beds of begonias round the soft, bluish statue of Michael the Archangel, the great central lime tree, the white stones leading up to Our Lady's Grotto, the handsome face of Fitzgerald the gardener – and then the wide porch, with old beggar women mumuring – I remember the progression, and the sound of the bell, and wondering which parlour

Sister Philomena would put me into – I liked the one on the left, with Bishop O'Dwyer's portrait and the dark upholstery.

When Fan was a child in Kilfinane she was not expected to live long; she was the "delicate" one, and neighbours thought, and said, "They'll never raise her. If the creature gets to fourteen years it'll be a wonder." Thus, great and anxious care was spent on her by her parents, by her loving young sisters, by the family doctor, and by specialists in Cork. Among the Little Women she was Beth; but unlike Beth she did not die. She made fourteen, against the betting; and lived for seventy-one more years as an indomitable and vigorous invalid. A warning, if you like, that it is wise to take very great care of children.

I suppose it was "consumption", as they called tuberculosis, that was mainly feared for the small Fan; and indeed she may have manifested symptoms – her brother was to die of it in his thirties, hurrying it on with alcoholism. She was almost certainly anaemic; also highly nervous, excitable and easily distressed. She was to be all of the last three as and when she pleased throughout her life.

It was sad and ironic for her, the delicate "pet", that her sisters had to leave her so long on the bleak shore alone. For fifty years she had to do with just remembering Katty, and telling us about her; and for more than a quarter of a century she had no sisters at all. Indeed, bereft of Mary in the convent it is remarkable that she survived. But she was already then elderly, and because of her eccentricities and her lazy charm, a community pet. And gradually she became the historian and the indulged doyenne of the house. Had Mother Margaret Mary, her strong-minded, intelligent sister – a real nun – died say ten years earlier than she did, it is conceivable that Fan might have gone mad.

For when in morbid girlhood she announced her decision to follow Mary and be a nun with her, Mother – that is, their sister Katty – questioned the idea anxiously – as well anyone might. Fan was not, physically or mentally, material for the life of rule and austerity. She was pious, but probably had no vocation to the religious life, and from her cradle had been allowed to go her ways and indulge her nerves and whims. Granted it must have been difficult to picture Fan in the ordinary life of the world – in marriage and passion and childbirth; but probably Katty said to herself that after all there was no need for her to marry; she could be a happy and pampered spinster. On the other hand, to try to be a nun – in a very austere and hardworked order?

Fan cut through all psychological thickets, however. She made no claims for her vocation and broke into no ecstasies. Simply she insisted that she could only face life where Mary was; she could be no longer separated from Mary – and so she was going to be a nun where Mary was a nun. That was the sum total of her purpose – its whole content. And no one could find an argument against it.

It is curious that Aunt Mary did not know how to deflect the timid wilfulness. She who while still a young nun was to be a most successful Mistress of Novices, who was a natural judge of human material, and had decidedly some of the governing talents of Teresa of Avila, must have known, with two years' experience of Presentation life, that her sister Fan should stay outside the walls and forgo the vows.

One does not know what she said or thought. Fan had her way, and settled to live – no matter what the conditions – where Mary was.

Mary may have been wiser than we know. Instinct

may have told her that Fan's escapism was her only safety; that if she was allowed to feel protected outside her own wilfulness, if she felt sure of the one person whom she ever sought to obey, she would be all right – and would even grow wise, and holy. As in her fashion she did.

At home there used to be two photographs of Mary and of Fan. Each had been done by the best photographer in Cork, ceremonially, before each girl left for the convent. That is to say, Mary's picture was of 1886, and Fan's of 1888. They were framed in simple gilt, and pleasantly mounted in white and gold; they were profile-neck-and-shoulders pictures, laid ghostly against dead white. I think they were what the photographer would have called "tinted", but, to give him his due, this adornment was hardly perceptible. The two girls would appear to have been wearing identical dark, high-necked dresses, with identical little hard collars showing, and identical cameo brooches. This cannot have been so. The plentiful hair of each, brushed very severely, was swept into a heavy chignon on the nape of each neck. That probably was so.

What hopelessly bad photographs! I often stared at them in wonder when I was a child; because they were representations of two twin and gloomy matrons of forty; whereas twenty, twenty-five and thirty years on from their dates, I knew these two faces of Mary and Fan, still young, restless and sharply differentiated – and if Mary's the more beautiful, still both beyond question the living, changing faces of women who could only have been vividly beautiful girls. When I was older I used to wonder what Grandfather had made of such absurd reminders of two who had fled girlhood while it was still so fresh and pliant in them.

Girlhood – yes, it was from that, from all with

which it bothered her and towards which its bright course led that Fan ran away, to enclosing vows and the protection of Mary. I do not believe that she ever had a sexual fright, or knew at all, in the simplest terms of experience, a recognisable sensual impulse. No boy in Kilfinane, at the dancing-class or on a picnic, would have dared a sentimental brush with one so standoffish and so fragile as Fanny Thornhill. Yet we can be sure, from the flight to the convent, and from the hysterics and commotions that for long years tormented her cloistered life, and vicariously the life of her cool and patient sister Mary – the "scruples", the tears, the interminable confessions, the fixed invalidism – that Fan was abnormally afraid of a region of sensual life which she would never enter, could not recognise, on which all her conscious self turned blinded eyes; but which nevertheless she knew with terror.

This is journeyman psychiatry. Fan might have been responsive to psycho-analysis – yet, to what purpose? To make her into a more useful member of her community, to train her to carry her weight, to give her a sense of proportion. Excellent, maybe. But the old way – years of striving within an acknowledged rule, years of facing the chill exactitudes of the confessional, years of consolatory reliance on the natural human love she took from her clear-minded sister – these did not turn Fan into an ordinary, dutiful nun indeed, but they brought her to sagacity and to a kind of holy gratitude, and as she had always been humble of spirit, and gracious and amusing when she chose – she became when it was too late to be ordinarily useful a refreshing original in community life, a cheerful counsellor to whom younger nuns became happily attached – and she grew to be holy, and I think not afraid any more of death or of God – or of any of the unknown darknesses.

But from cradle to grave, Fan's open and expressible preoccupation – a covering for all that lay in the unconscious or in the hinterland of the darkly glimpsed – was health, or ill-health, her own, and at a remove everyone else's. As we have seen, this was not her fault; the subject was indeed forced on her at the baptismal font when, she told me, she did not open her mouth or utter a sound; so that her godmother said afterwards – lifting no doubt a rich glass of port to her lips – that the little girl would have many sicknesses and a short life.

She had some moral tales about health. One of the best, which cost Fan's reticence much to tell, was of Miss Agatha O'Reilly of Kilfinane. (The story is as true as that Fan was certain of it, but the name of the unlucky heroine was not, be sure, the name I give her here.) Our hearing it arose from this: we children on feast days or special days were permitted to stay long hours "in the parlour" with our aunts. We loved to do so, because we were spoiled there, running wild in the kitchen garden and among the lovely chicken runs, allowed to play the piano, and sometimes to examine the treasures of the sacristy – and stuffed all the time with refreshments – puff cracknels, Madeira cake, milk and pears and all delights. And on these days of caper we were granted use of the Chaplain's lavatory – a very convenient retreat in a corridor near the sacristy. Fan, observant and very anxious when we were running wild on the outer edges of the convent, noticed that some of us never seemed to go to the Chaplain's lavatory. This worried her until she did not know what to do. She foresaw dreadful troubles for us if we did not go to the lavatory. So in the end some of us were told – separately, of course – and I for one, what happened to Agatha O'Reilly.

When Fan was a child in Kilfinane if a person of substance wanted a day of pleasure – to attend a matinée, for instance, or to buy a ball dress; to consult a specialist, have a photograph taken, or make a General Confession – or to do all of these things – he or she went to Cork for a day.

It was an expedition well within the compass of the active. At about seven in the morning the excursionist mounted the *Long Car* (Biaconi's famous Cars) in the Square. This took him to Kilmallock in the valley, where he caught a train to Mallow, where he changed into the down express from Dublin to Cork. With ordinary luck he would be in Cork at eleven o'clock, had a glorious day of pleasure and business before him, and at about eight in the evening would mount the up express and cover the morning journey in reverse – to reach home with parcels and tales of the road after midnight.

One day the O'Reillys were going in a group on this elaborate outing. There was some fuss about the early morning tea, the clock was discovered to be slow, and the males who were travelling suddenly began to stampede. The Long Car was in the Square! Agatha had run upstairs for her last preparations when there were shouts from below. One can hear them. "For God's sake, Agatha! Come on, will you?" And she did come on, snatching up her gloves and her purse – flew to the roar of her brother. She had not got to the lavatory or the commode or whatever the O'Reillys had.

The day went according to pattern – a very fine and successful day. Agatha was a bit uncomfortable, but she was young, and she believed she would find an opportunity, in one or other of the hotels. But in the 'seventies and 'eighties of the last century ladies, once outside their own hall doors, were assumed to be angels, and no provision whatever was made for a primary physical need – even in capital cities. So in the Irish provinces, if a modest country girl was away from her own house for a whole day, it is understandable that she could go through agonies of discomfort. She would not go wandering by herself to the upper floors of hotels, she could not possibly ask a brother or a father what she was to do; she could only suffer and hope and despair – until at last the anguish might seem to die in her. She would have passed the point of crisis, by some kind of miracle – and the latter part of the misery would just be misery: inertia, stony endurance.

All of this happened to Agatha O'Reilly. She suffered that whole day in Cork and the long journey home, and was scolded contemptuously by her brother for being so dull, so ungracious, no fun at all – after all the shopping and spending.

They got to Kilfinane at midnight, with the parcels and the presents. Agatha was almost too tired then to crawl upstairs before supper. But she did. And then she lay down on her bed and felt very sick and strange. Her mother came looking for her, and she told her she couldn't go down to supper, that she must sleep.

She did sleep. But, according to Fan, she woke the next morning a lunatic, and she never regained her reason.

That was an effective story. I can see Fan now, forcing her reticence aside in her need to frighten us to the lavatory.

She could have been a good teacher, and was for many years, maybe still is, remembered affectionately by ladies of Limerick, now themselves advanced in age, who began their attack on the three Rs under her cool blue eyes and impatient baton. But conditions of elementary teaching in her young days were harsh indeed; she had no technical training and it was her life-long habit to be ill and incapable when she felt ill and incapable. Brought up as she was it could hardly have occurred to Fan that a sane person, feeling the onset of some headache or sweat or disorder, could do other than down tools at once, down blinds as well, and give full attention to the symptom of malaise.

Thus from her beginnings she was an erratic and unreliable presence in the classrooms of Sexton Street, and my impression is that in her middle age, when we began to know her properly, she no longer did more than occasional substitute work in the school. Certainly I remember her only as an invalid, large in shawls; and that when one visited the convent it was touch and go as to whether Fan would be well enough to come to the parlour. But she so greatly loved Katty's children, if only for the reason that such we were, that she had to be feeling low indeed when she did not make her way to us, to the parlour window and the sunshine.

She could be fun then: tyrannical, fussy, inquisitorial – and great fun.

Aunt Annie was not afraid of Fan, as she was a shade, I think, of Aunt Mary. One could be. And she was comically afraid of Auntie Mick – which was natural. But Fan and she were easy together and gave battle freely. Often I have seen them in angry tears, glaring at each other across the parlour window; but Aunt Mary might be present, or would hurry in delighted to have snatched a few more minutes with Annie – and she would scatter their Tweedledum-Tweedledee fury with some quick sweep of amused reproach. They both always did whatever Mary said, and if she told them to stop fighting they stopped. For the time being.

When Aunt Annie came to visit us in Limerick, the first certainty of the first day was that she, her accompanying little daughters, Moira and Jen, and one or other of us – the time being school holidays – visited the convent, and stayed to luncheon there. The thing was to get Aunt Annie dressed cap-à-pie and ready to leave the house at a quarter to twelve. She would have talked imperiously to whom among us she could get to stay her course – usually Nance or Tom or me – until far into the small hours. While she dealt with her breakfast tray, one or other of us would come loafing in again, to pick up the conversation, lounging at the foot of her bed. I can see her now – the smocked nightgown, the mischievous, happy eyes, the head of curlers. But warnings came up – did we know it was half past ten? – and she had to be left to battle with her curling tongs, which she loved to clatter and wave about in menace, and with which she ruined her hair. On to the end she would not forgo the Alexandra curls of youth. We got her to the convent gate in fair enough time – Eric or Jack in charge of some superb harness-cob in a high round trap – and much comedy about how dangerously they drove, and would they stop instantly please, and let her walk in peace to Sexton Street.

Then there was the parade up the long visitors' garden, past St Michael, and Our Lady's Grotto – and as we were expected we knew that Fan was lurking behind the parlour windows, inspecting us all in a mixed fever of hot love and cold criticism. Every move and detail of our advance was under the savage eye of her devotion.

Well – we were in our Sunday best, and could do no more. To the dickens with Fan. If she didn't like us she could tell us to go away – and we'd all go down town to Miss Smith's for a fine luncheon. This flourish from Aunt Annie, who, looking very pretty and bright-eyed, had already started to wave to her spying white-guimped sister behind the lace curtains.

In the hall and, more visible in the sunlit parlour, there were some dash-away tears on the faces of the two reunited ones – easily managed by Fan with a large checked handkerchief, but Annie had to roll back her spotted net veil. Then there was a whirling reception for Moira and Jen, two very attractive fair-haired children. (Aunt Mary told me that Mother used to say to them: "Now look, Annie will be visiting you next week with her two little girls – so will you please keep quiet about *my* children during her visit! It's very annoying for her, when she brings hers such a long way to see you, and you *will* keep talking on about mine.") Mother was perfectly right. Fan could be more heavy-footed than an elephant; so although she adored the young MacCarthys, if she did happen to get deflected on to any news of Katty's children – whom, I think, she did not always clearly see, but rather dreamt – she found no irrelevance in boring the unconcerned or annoying the jealous with long talk of us.

Scenes in the convent parlour, so many and variously angled, some crowded with figures, others flat and badly grouped; occasional passages of tension or muffled drama which minor players did not always understand; moments sometimes of sheer woe and heavy tears; and large moods of fun, everyone eating and drinking and getting flushed, and singing solos at the upright piano; various strange nuns, short and tall, in and out with great double kisses, much exclamation – these do not compose easily, although Fan played a strong lead in all of them, and they had unbroken unity of place. Perhaps too they had a kind of time-unity, in that the ideas, sentiments and beliefs that prevailed throughout them – in terms of the world – were those of a simple country girl who had walked out of that world in 1888, and who still persisted in being very busy with it from behind her high wall.

Yes – time and the world stood still in that parlour; or else obeyed Fan and moved as she directed. And it was the wilfulness of the leading lady, and her wordly tussles in her parlour with the worlds of others that made hours spent with her so lively, tricky and memorable. For she would have the world, at least that small part of it in which her beloved ones moved and in which she would have sought to guide our every step – she would have that world a simple and safe and tightly-organised space, within which we, all her relatives large and small, shone and dazzled and succeeded and were happy and good and always out of harm's and temptation's way; and so she could not rest, because even she could see, and sharply, that our world was not so arranged – any more than anyone else's.

But still, she wanted it that way; and to the end she fussed against reality, for others. *She* had evaded it.

Aunt Annie carried no armour at all against hard facts, and in her later life she was the victim of her pure inability to deal with specific ones among them, those of shop-keeping especially, of money and its lack. But she acknowledged their existence; after all, she had to. And she could sometimes speak sharply about them, but only for a sentence or two, as if to relieve feelings she seldom showed, exposing small chinks in her bright courage. She liked to forget, or to seem to forget, as far as possible, complexities and dangers which she could neither understand nor alter. And she believed in letting people alone; above all, she did not plague the self-conscious young – rather, she had some grace for setting them at ease.

This Fan had not. Devotion deprived her of ease. We all had to be wonderful, radiant, happy, superbly intelligent and marvellously well-dressed. So she dreamt us, and so night and day she prayed for us. So she envisaged us in absence, and so she looked forward to us when we were coming to visit her. We were perfect, and we had to be seen to be perfect – especially by any stray member of the Presentation community. And that mania was what Aunt Annie was thrusting off when she said, so consolingly to us young: "To the dickens with Fan. We're in our Sunday best, and if she doesn't like us she can tell us to go away."

And of course we were hardly seated round her by the window when excited, adoring Fan began to see, by this sad sign and that, that we were not perfect, not yet anyway; and that our world had traps and catches in it. A child might have a sore lip, or be wearing a hat that Fan found unbecoming; or the features of some one of us disappointed her – she had remembered So-and-So as prettier. Any sensitive person, even when very young, could watch the creeping of disappointment and worry into Fan's welcoming face as those unmanageable details in us hurtled against her dream. Nothing critical would be said at first; but all would be said in the end, and we were very lucky if someone was not wretchedly upset. Because unfortunately we were all as Thornhill as Fan in being most easily upset.

"Oh, the pets – they're lovely, Annie, God bless them! Such golden hair! Jen, my pet – you're the image of your mother! And how do you like school, Moira darling? Go on, Annie – tell me all the news! How are the boys? Are you sure that that nurse is trustworthy?" (Aunt Annie had left two small sons at home in Fermoy.)

Aunt Annie answered merrily and happily.

"It's very good of Willie to spare you to us for a while. And you're looking grand yourself! Not stout at all – you must mind not to get stout, Annie..."

"You're a fine one to talk!"

"Oh well, I can't help it – with the way my health is always, and all the milk I have to take. Is that a new suit you've on?"

"Yes, I got it in Cork before Christmas. Do you like it?" said Aunt Annie, boldly riding for trouble.

"Well, turn round. Yes – it's a good fit on the shoulders. Nice quality material too. But – is that colour the fashion now?"

It was clear that Aunt Annie's new suit was a disappointment to Fan – and this made us sad. But the only way in which to cheer her up over any failure she felt to have been made about an article of dress was to persuade her that anyone wearing it was a leader of fashion.

"The very height," said Aunt Annie. "There's hardly any other shade to be bought in Mrs Fitzsimon's this season."

Mrs Fitzsimon's of Cork was, as Fan knew, the leading ladies' shop in all Munster at that time. It was improbable that the outfit now under criticism had been bought there, but the half-lie brought consolation into Fan's eyes.

"Ah well, if you tell me that! Still – it's not really your colour, Annie – "

"And I've always thought that black isn't yours," from Annie affectionately.

Such a breeze was nothing; but it showed that the wind sat in the prevailing quarter.

On Aunt Annie's first day at the convent when she came to Limerick the parlour took the excited to-and-fro of other members of the Community besides her two sisters. There would be later visits when she would sit alone with Mary or Fan or both, and with only one or none of us for escort. But the first day was a kind of gala, and this nun and that got permission to have a few minutes with Mrs MacCarthy – so that there was a great swirling in and out of the side door of black robes and white guimpes. Chief and first as a rule came Sister Bernardine, Annie's schoolmate in Kilfinane, youngest of those O'Deas whom grandfather did not approve. Also there was a pair of sisters – sisters in blood, I mean – who held some remote cousinship to the Thornhills, a link invisible indeed, for the two were as plain, not to say ugly, of face – God bless the holy women! – as the Thornhills were handsome. Sister Benignus too, young, good-looking, intelligent – I remember that she used to come to salute Annie MacCarthy on some pretext or other.

We children benefited from all this commotion, because the nuns were very kind to us, paid us compliments and always produced some novelty from their wide sleeves – a holy picture, a coloured pencil, an apple or a pear. And we got quite expert at the kiss on both cheeks and occasional clash with guimpe or headdress. Many members of the Community had rough-skinned faces, and one or two were downright bristly – but not Bernardine or Benignus, and not by any means Aunt Mary or Aunt Fan. Aunt Fan indeed was exquisite to kiss.

Bernardine and Annie greeted each other always with great pleasure, and memories of silly, irresponsible days they had known in the lost village of childhood carried them in light communion of their present selves. The two were humorists, and if Bernardine was the more sceptical Annie had a benevolence and scope outside the nun's reach. But, for all their trust in the long sympathy of innocent years, the two women must secretly have wondered in that parlour, each at the other's strangeness. Yet all that either had done was to grow up from the clearly identifiable green shoot that she had been. Each had changed only to become herself.

Bernardine, slender and swift-moving, had a very interesting but not a beautiful face. There were eccentricities in it that in a sense equalled beauty, and when I was a child I used to think it one of the most complicated faces there could be. Looking back, seeing that dark, worked-upon mask with greater clarity now, I think I was right.

This nun resembled Fan in being unsuited to the life she had elected. Like Fan she was very holy and she had not the latter's wilfulness; she had wretched health all through her life, was troubled, anxious and full of scruples, like Fan; she was highly strung and the prey of her nerves; but, unlike Fan, she was energetic, she required to be energetic, even in extreme fatigue. When Bernardine was at the end of all her rope, she still desired to be in life, to be with people and to be doing her work.

Fan, on the contrary, never got to the end of her rope, because before it was reached she needed to withdraw from life, from people and from work. She required absolute rest, and she took it. They were the two spectacular near-invalids of the convent in the years when I knew it best. But they were sharply contrasted, and it is odd that the two *frileuses sensibles* came from the same small, bleak Irish village.

The words *frileuse* and *sensible* may seem exotic indeed for use in the Presentation parlour in Limerick. Yet there unconsciously I learnt their meanings. There I learnt – from watching more than Aunts Annie and Fan, but many other women and a few girls; men too, my father and one or two priests, and my own young brothers – such intricacies and involutions of human feeling, so much of its confusions, clouds and lights, intangibles of pleasure and disappointment; sensed so many of the traps and false leads that hem about affection; so often winced for blind cuts against poor, vulnerable self-esteem; in fact, assisted so repeatedly in childhood and youth at what may be symbolised as a kind of long ballet of the smile and the tear, a serialised ballet, choreographed impromptu by the unconscious of all performers, and danced to the music of rapid speech, low voices, and songs sung at the yellow-keyed piano in the corner – so repeatedly was I a part of this unusual variety performance in my most open-eyed and receptive years that to revisit it in maturity, as often by chance of memory or reference I do, is to be invaded all over again, at least in a great part of my sensibilities, by the unknowingness and the unbalanced young anxiety which were dominant in me, I think, through most of those Parlour enactments. A visitation which is so strong and unmanageable as to make it seem impossible to apprehend the vivid sequences of comedy and grief and farce, and to shape them into a consistent whole. For instead of being the producer now, as I should be, of the muddled, fleeting, changeful drama, I seem to become again a mere and small and uninformed crowd-actor, shuffling about uneasily down stage left – and always got up in uncomfortable Sunday clothes.

Yet that parlour was a place where my aunts – all five of them – were to be seen, to be observed in action in twos or threes, and always in relation to us and the anxieties and pleasures which we caused in them. So I have to struggle with the unresting scene, with its deceptive lights and changes. But always the mood there is of sensibility overriding sense; and were

I to enter that parlour now, where Bishop Butler and Bishop O'Dwyer still frown from the walls, where the piano is still out of tune, but into which none of those who made it so rich and memorable a place will ever come whirling again to greet me, I know that I would face it as in the past, excited and wondering and with all my nerves exposed. And, *de rigueur*, in my best clothes!

Clothes, alas, personal appearances had much, far too much to do with setting up states of hyper-sensibility in the parlour. The community almost to a nun, even to our wise, relatively wise, Aunt Mary, was exceedingly interested in the figures cut by all their visitors; and as we, the O'Briens and MacCarthys were considered – certainly by Fan and possibly by Aunt Mary – to outshine and overtop in our least aspects any other imaginable relative or visitor of any other nun, and as some of the nuns played up to this legend, the strain of such idealisation was hard on us, and too often a savage anxiety for Fan. Mother had disliked being first presented to Father with a strip of sticking plaster across the bridge of her nose; but that was mere fun compared with the hundreds of times when I, for one, did all I could, in vain, to get out of calling at the convent – if, say, I had a sty on my eye, or an unfortunate new hat, or had just returned from Kilkee in an over-freckled condition. We were white-and-thin-skinned children whose faces freckled and peeled, but did not bronze or turn to angel gold. These frecklings worried Father very much, and he used to plague us with preventives, useless, and with messy night-cures, applications of carrot juice and cream – worse than useless; but he at least was kind to our embarrassment, and did not discuss our afflictions in public.

To Fan, however, our blemishes were all-but-unbearable; and she never bore anything in silence.

"The child is destroyed, Tom! Why on earth couldn't you make her wear a sun-hat?"

And the child felt destroyed, and slinked away from solemn Fan.

AUNT MARY

Aunt Mary began her religious life with a decision and an action which placed her, simple girl as she was, among the tiresome and self-centred saints.

The innocent Thornhill family was united in tenderness and sentiment. The parents were guilelessly in love with their four daughters and their one fragile son. All of this group were content, even if tremulously, that Katty, their darling, was to marry Tom O'Brien on some convenient day before Advent. Splendid. Terrible too. But beautiful Katty would have to marry – and here was the occasion and the gay and gracious lover. No use wincing, no use dreading the natural, right course of human life.

But Mary, more beautiful perhaps than Katty – that was always a question, and one could see why – Mary already in love with God, was to cast sadness over the simple, happy occasion. She saw and chose for herself an act of mortification. Since she loved Katty so much but loved God more, she would offer up to God all the pain and pleasure she would have had in being a part of the whole family experience of Katty's wedding. Simply before it took place she would depart from all she loved, and enter the Presentation House in Limerick. It was the first sacrifice she would make of her human desires; it was immense – so immense that one suspects it relieved her troubled breast to settle for it.

Her parents could not understand her harsh decision. If Katty was hurt I do not know; but I believe that she must have been bewildered when her nearest, her beautiful companion-sister, her friend in everything, insisted on that sharp good-bye, and sped away to the lonely postulancy of a cold, silent rule rather than wait to befriend the wedding eve, and stand bridesmaid at the communion rails. Katty forgave her, we can be sure. She forgave everyone – did she admit the condescending word.

Father used to tell of the fun he had in that late summer of 1886 when once or twice Mary Thornhill came to Limerick for the day, to interview her future Reverend Mother, arrange for her convent trousseau and so on. She seems to have made her trips unaccompanied, and Father took charge of her in his native city. His engagement to a beautiful girl from the hinterland of east Limerick had been announced; and here he was now, dashing about in his high gig, very gay with a very beautiful coppery-haired young woman who was presented, when absolutely necessary, to this or that one as "Miss Thornhill of Kilfinane."

"They were all envying me," Father used to say. "They were staggered by Mary – and why wouldn't they be! And yet, the joke was that I still had the ace up my sleeve!"

I wonder what they talked about, Father and Mary Thornhill, as he met her train, gave her lunch, drove her to her convent, showed her the sights of Limerick, and then saw her off at evening for Kilfinane where his Katty waited for her. He was always for gaiety, even in later life against the odds. When he was young and in love he must have been eagerly high-spirited, and he always delighted in beautiful women and in quick wits. Aunt Mary, when I knew her in her days of maturity and high office, as Mistress of Novices and as Reverend Mother, was very beautiful and had quick wits; but these wits had been trained in experience by then – experience of women and children in novitiate and school; and of men – priests, doctors, school inspectors and bishops – in convent government. But the twenty-year-old country girl who was wilfully indulging herself in self-sacrifice in that emotionally charged summer of 1886 had a long way to go and everything to learn. And one can be sure that Father thought it both mad and unkind of her to insist on becoming a nun a mere month or so before Katty's wedding. So I have imagined that the gay drives about Limerick, showing off one Thornhill beauty to the questioning citizens, may not have been all that so gay; may indeed have contained their moments of awkwardness and even of pain. But Father was not a man to record such against anyone he loved – or even in secret, if he could help it, to remember them.

So all he told us about was his proud joke; I can imagine tension.

Aunt Mary was clean-cut for a vocational life. Into whatever race or class she was born she would naturally have found herself to be its servant, or the servant of God. She desired to spend herself, to be used, to work her passage. She thought that the natural thing was to give to life, and she never thought at all about receiving. Her first selfishness in sacrifice was only an error of exaggeration, of overstatement. In young passion of abnegation she had not yet a way of measuring. Discipline and vows were what she needed – and she ran to find them. Father may have thought that more likely she needed an ardent and skilful suitor, but I believe he would have been wrong. I believe that Aunt Mary was a natural-born nun, and more than that, a natural-born governor of nuns.

It was as such that I knew her.

As she flashed in and out of the parlour she was all speed and grace. The slimmest nun imaginable and, when I remember her, with a face of exaggerated beauty. Eyes like hard-cut sapphires and all her person lean and quick and clean-edged. If she was very holy – and it is sure she was – she seemed to throw that grace over her shoulder in company, where she was as gentle and ordinary as she could manage. But she was not ordinary – and so it was not easy for a child or a young girl who perceived that to be at ease with her.

Her sisters, however, took her on the swing. Fan was calm with Mary because Mary was calm, just precisely calm, for Fan. Without Mary there had been only the world and its terrors; here in the convent had always been Mary, and that meant calm for Fan, and all the more calm if Mary was actually in the same room with her.

Aunt Annie may have been occasionally set back by Mary – perhaps because the latter's sense of humour was in a different group from hers. But I do not think that she was afraid of her, for all her respect. Mary was after all her very sister; and Aunt Annie was blessed in all her warm loves in that her ironic spirit simply denied pedestals to living creatures. Her loves were for that torrentially and easily giving, where they were given; because she expected no impossibilities. And when withheld, it was only with a wondering smile. Aunt Annie was in fact no judge; but all those other aunts were, I think, in their up-and-down measures. Most people are, indeed. Hardly ever does one meet the comfort of one who is a natural non-judge. In a long life I can recall of such only Aunt Annie.

Aunt Mary had a soldierly quality, and was naturally

a controller of events and persons. As quite a young nun she was elected to the various officeships of the religious life, from sacristan to Bursar, to Mistress of Novices.

When she was still quite young there took place, as every five years by the Presentation Rule, an election for the office of Reverend Mother. This was by secret ballot of the community, and took place in prayer and silence in the Choir of the Chapel. The Bishop of Limerick presided over the ceremony, and was assisted by the chaplain. Each nun knelt in her stall, and after prayers and blessings in the presence of the Blessed Sacrament the Bishop counted the votes, and pronounced the elected nun.

This time it was Aunt Mary.

"Margaret Mary Thornhill," said his lordship.

Fan leapt from her stall with a scream.

"Oh no, no, no!" she sobbed. "Not Mary! She can't! She mustn't! Not Mary, my Lord!"

I suppose that nuns on either side took hold of her, and replaced her in her stall; but I believe that Mary, standing up, tall and tense, to go to the Bishop's feet and accept her duty, just turned a second and smiled affectionately at Fan.

Responsibility was an idea wholly terrible to Fan. One can see her point. Responsibility *is* terrible. But to the responsibly-minded it is not so terrible as to the imaginative. And Fan – of a certain kind of imagination practically all compact – had watched with terror her sister's climb through the offices of her order. When Mary, young and cool, was elected Mistress of Novices – a responsibility indeed – Fan could not for months, she used to tell us, get a wink of sleep at all, for terror before her vision of Mary's duties. Yet this was the same Fan who knew very well – for she was no fool – that she herself could not have pulled through her novitiate had it not been for guidance from the side-lines of a sister only two years older and just emerged herself, in black veil, from the troublesome arena of the white veils. Fan knew in fact that she was a professed and well-behaved nun because Mary was an especially gifted one, and very particularly able for the offices she had to assume.

Aunt Mary got on like a house on fire, as they say, with men. I say this of her with perfect ease, and shall have more to say of it. It was an innocent power, a grace which life in office required her to use without knowing that she did so, and which was nowhere touched or stained by sexual idea. She was beautiful; she was witty in a simple fashion; certainly she was quick in the uptake, and whether she grew aware of this or not with experience I do not know but in ordinary commerce she understood men. Bishop, chaplain, gardener, embarrassed young doctor, pompous school inspector, visiting prelate, visiting schoolboy, lonely, mourning brother-in-law – Mary talked to any of them directly to their purpose. She could make men laugh, and want to go on talking to her.

I watched her much when I was a child, so I know what I mean about her. And it is when I reflect back to that power which I watched her exercise that now I see her relationship to Teresa of Avila. I am not suggesting that my humble and humbly educated aunt was as she lived as great as the sixteenth-century genius. Heavens and absurdity, how could she be? However, I do think this, that had Aunt Mary been one of the three or four ignorant and gallant young nuns who bravely went with the mad-seeming Teresa in Avila from the decaying house of *El Encarnación* up the hill and across the town to the little house to be called *San José* and now *de las Madres* – and I believe that indeed she would have gone with Teresa – then, she might well have become one of the Saint's greatest Prioresses of the Reform. I mean that. I think Aunt Mary had what those young women had who were to govern Beas and Toledo and Sevilla in the letter and spirit of the Saint's fiery desires.

It is a high claim to make for a blood relation! But this blood relation had a lonely quality. It was not as simple as pure holiness, although I know that she was a very holy woman; it was an austere and happy kind of indifference to herself, a simple humility which escaped that self-consciousness, that touchiness which was a general plague of our breed – on both sides, I'd say – for Father was as much its prey as any Thornhill. If Aunt Mary was an unsuspected and unselfconscious saint I do not know; but to the simplest child it was clear that she held herself as nothing, save as the servant of Him to whom she had given her human life. This clarity of intention in her made her, little as she would have guessed such a thing, formidable; it made her seem sometimes ruthless or at least impatient. But she was impatient only over trifles; no one who was impatient before humanity's real weaknesses, our shadowy selfish queries and agitations, could have been the legendary successful Mistress of Novices that Aunt Mary became, could have been so calm and commanding a Reverend Mother, or could have guided such a character as Fan, in calm love, through the all but impossible proposition of the religious life.

She believed of course in prayer. She heard God's voice in all her days and nights; and it never occurred to her that character, sheer character, was doing for her always and in everything whatever she asked for at early Mass or at evening Benediction. Yet it is my belief that if by some unimaginable accident Aunt Mary had woken up one morning to an absence of

God, to discovering herself without that governing idea, and supposedly finding that her mind was empty of it and quite calmly blank instead of filled with the incontrovertible vision of this personal reality and attention to her prayers – it is my belief that such a blackout could have altered in nothing her isolatedly holy character. Her person was holy – God or no God – in that it was given to service of life. I think that in any society, Christian, pagan, rationalist, communist or what you will, she would have been as I knew her – naturally at ease in indifference to herself, and naturally at the service of others. And always, in any society, she would have been invulnerable, indifferent before the temptations of the flesh.

This guesswork about a truly very beautiful nun may not make her seem endearing; and I for one could never warm to her as I did, in different degrees, to her younger sisters, Annie and Fan. But the world as it came to her loved her; and she could manage the world, as I have said. And she could indeed manage nuns, no matter how hysterically they adored her.

I am only guessing now; I shall never understand Aunt Mary. Because, without contradiction of any claim I have made, she was as worldly as Fan. For others, as Fan did, she sought and desired success and money and fur coats and glory. For others – her nieces and nephews, Katty's and Annie's children – she quite absurdly wanted all she had herself cast off. And being a more measured and shrewd person than Fan – I hardly think more intelligent, because Fan had imagination and a kind of flair all her own – but Mary, in active touch with the world through her offices of government, knew what Fan did not know about manoeuvres for place and money – and so in their worldly dreams and plottings for us the elder sister was the more troublesome. Also, I always found her worldliness somehow more shocking than dear Fan's. Fan was a dreamer, and really very silly. Aunt Mary was no such thing.

She had great charm, whether she knew that or not. And a boyish, mischievous manner – indeed, a spirit of mischief. When she was a young nun, Sister Sacristan, she had charge of a certain small shrine of St Joseph, in the corridor which led to the sacristy. Like Teresa of Avila, of whom I imagine she had never heard, Aunt Mary had a strong devotion to this saint. In Teresa I have always found this devotion odd. Joseph was no doubt a good man, but his record is dim, and I have always wondered why on earth the great Avilan believed him to be always at the ready to hear her stormy and impossible requests. However, Aunt Mary had the same idea about him, took great care of his shrine, and prayed to him very much – asking him for this and that worldly boon for Mother or Aunt Annie, or Grandfather. So, for some very special intention – it may have been for Father to sell some bloodstock extra well at Newmarket, or for Uncle Willie to make a good wine contract with the new regiment at Glanworth, or for Uncle Pat *not* to make the marriage he was envisaging – anyway for some purely worldly wish for others she had made a fervent and zealous novena of prayers to St Joseph, covering his shrine in the meantime with flowers, and paying him manifold, candle-lit attentions.

She was disappointed in whatever her demand was. St Joseph did not yield results. So she addressed him angrily, took his statue and turned its face to the wall.

This was an insolent thing to do – and of course by evening it had been reported to Reverend Mother. Sister Sacristan was severely rebuked, and had to replace the saint in his proper position.

"I was annoyed," she said. "He deserved it. He

should have stayed the way he was until tomorrow."

Such simplicity will bore sophisticated readers – yet, what they will find hard to believe is this, that were Aunt Mary by chance their hostess in the Presentation Parlour, for sherry or lunch or what you will, they would have found her their match in all moves of conversation – accepted and polite moves, I mean.

Certainly she was effective in the Parlour. When she entered it grew bright. She came in at speed, but her hurry was as if on a rush of wings, for she was very graceful. Veils and rosary beads flying never brushed to disturb against anything. But that is a trick many nuns have, as also they have the secret of looking immaculate, and cool. Huge, floating encasements of starched linen, pleated and tight-fitting folds of dark cloth, leather girdles, heavy crucifixes swinging from polished rosaries of bead – in this armour they swirl about winter and summer, uniformly adjusted to weather and circumstances as if they walked naked, or as the women of India walk through London rain and slush, undisturbed in complicated saris of silk.

Aunt Mary, if she was an example of the well-groomed and easy kind of nun, was only one out of many I have observed throughout the world. One marvels at the accent of their un-made-up faces, tightly bound in linen; at hands which seem massaged and manicured, yet most certainly are not; above all, the wonder is for the expanses of virgin linen, never limp, never stained – even as they dash and splash through our common life, as now so many, many of them do.

Fan would gloom if one called on her without notice. "Not even giving me time to change my *guimpe*," she would say and would point with contempt to a breastplate so morning-white as to hurt the eyes.

But all of this in passing.

Let me recall Aunt Mary in the Parlour. Christmas Day would be a good occasion. It was our first ceremony on that day, our first worldly ceremony, that is. We had all been to eight o'clock Mass at our parish church, St John's Cathedral. Father would have no going to midnight Mass. The riff-raff of the town was loose at that hour, he said, and he would not have his children meet it. And in the churches crowded by the poor and the dirty we might get fleas, or worse afflictions. Let him not be judged un-Christian for this – for he was not. He was only a clean-habited and affectionate man who wanted to keep us in good health and as long as possible unaware of violence and uproar in life. So instead of the fun and novelty of the midnight ceremonies we had the bleak morning rigours of ordinary Mass and Communion, fasting and frozen. The novelties were only the exquisite alto boy's voice in *Adeste Fideles* after the Consecration – and before the *Credo* there were the ten minutes of the Administrator's Christmas sermon. I have heard bad sermons all over the world, and I believe a good sermon to be the whitest of white blackbirds; I have listened only to two that I remember for merit. But for sheer agonising badness, flatness, inexcusable platitudinous fatuity those Christmas sermons from the various head priests of St John's Cathedral over my years of childhood and girlhood – and I was an attentive listener – take all the cakes and every imaginable biscuit. They were agonising, that is all I can say. And some of those flinty, dead, unholy voices I can hear now this minute, as I write.

Well, God has forgiven the well-meaning men, if I have not. And afterwards there was breakfast – wonderful and picturesque and decorated breakfast, with candles lighted and frilled cold dishes on the sideboard, and wrapped-up presents heaped at every place – and a deep sense of relief and benevolence.

Afterwards there came the campaign of the Parlour. On Christmas Day Aunts Mary and Fan held high reception for us from noon to three o'clock. And when Mary was in office, as Reverend Mother, as Mother Assistant or, again, as Reverend Mother, there was hardly question of our possession of the Large Parlour. (There were two lesser parlours – but neither was furnished with a piano.) However, even in all the many years when we belonged to the party in power, so to speak, there were awkward possibilities of protocol; a Monsignor or even a travelling bishop might visit his aunt or his sister on such a day – and throw all our importance out of count; or some titled person might arrive and cause Sister Lucy, the portress, to lose her head. You never knew. So, breakfast over, we younger ones were not given half enough time to brood over our presents; we had to be upstairs, changing into our newest and best, and setting off hours too early, "to bag the Parlour". This was Father's idea – and over such a matter this kindest of men was a tyrannical fusspot. So off we had to go, feeling fools, in dressed-up instalments, to take up our positions, much too soon for the aunts, in the Parlour.

Father himself, who took everything to do with Christmas with the most generous seriousness, would not leave the house until the post came. The sending of Christmas cards – and presents, may I add, for he was princely – but the sending of cards was only equalled in pleasurable seriousness for him by his reception of the cards and greetings of his friends – and of ours! (Useless to hope for a private message from anyone at Christmas. Father, in sheer pleasure, had to see and consider all that came to his house.) So he waited, alone, for the postman – who arrived intoxicated before one o'clock, and very certainly did not leave our house without some further cheer. Then, and only then, Father would have himself driven to the convent, and come smiling and waving up the long garden – I can see him now – with a Gladstone bag. Our Christmas post, which would be publicly and ruthlessly opened, by him and Fan and Auntie Mick and Sister Bernardine, in the Parlour – and thoroughly discussed and disputed and assessed, every silliest card of it.

"My old friend, William Hill – a nice card really – but I've known William choose better – "

Father, through his business and his friendliness, had many friends in England as well as in Ireland. He also chose a very handsome traditional horsey card for himself, had a great many of them engraved, and sent them punctually to such old friends as William Hill. I think that it was with this especial old friend that the comedy persisted for years of the exchange between them, besides cards, of a Limerick ham and a Stilton cheese. Now most people can eat ham – we must hope Mr Hill could – but Father could not stand cheese in any form, at any time. And as for Stilton! I always remember the amused groans at the arrival of this handsome Christmas present. What I cannot remember is what was done with the splendid Stilton.

However, back to the cards; back to the Parlour. A large, square Georgian room, with two fine broad windows giving on to the visitors' garden, two doors facing each other, one from the hall, the other through which the nuns came to us but beyond which we might not travel. A handsome Georgian fireplace. A tinny little piano. A number of comfortable but severe Victorian chairs. Plants in brass pots. Two portraits of two bishops of Limerick on the walls. (The Bishop of Limerick was always, *ex officio*, the governor of any Presentation house.) Some prints and engravings of religious subjects from old masters. A highly polished floor. A rep-covered Victorian sofa. A central table to which, on Christmas Day and other days, many kinds of refreshment were borne by Sister Lucy and Sister Philomena.

A very pleasant parlour. But on Christmas Day one could not see it very well, because by one o'clock it was thronged. Nine of us, Katty's children, for a start, ranging – let us take a date at random – from twenty years to five. That means that Mother – Katty – is more than five years dead, and that her name can at least be spoken without instant tears, between the elders. Nine of us fidgeting around; Father on the sofa with his Gladstone bag; Fan safely planted near him, between him and the window, cushioned, shawled and happy, as eager as dear Tom about the Christmas post in the opened bag. Auntie Mick, who will not stay long, across the window from Fan, upright and elegant, talking to Mother Liguori, and dealing very firmly with Gerard, the youngest of us whom she detests and who seems to love annoying her. He pulls and teases now at her exquisitely rolled and delicate silk umbrella; his fingers are chocolate-stained. But with Father so near she will not give him the brutal slap and insult that he would get on her own ground.

Music Ho! The little piano is overworked on Christmas Day. Our sister Clare, a teenager, is unable to bear the out-of-tuneness of it. She is a natural musician, and has absolute pitch. However, on Christmas Day she tries to control her impatience. Most of the family can sing, and if they can, today they must do so for the nuns.

Now, the funny thing is that, like our father who had a sweet, light tenor voice, most of our family could sing in tune, and with sufficient volume and taste to be bearable performers. But two, Clare and

Gerard, had in fact musical and singing talents of distinction. In the general Christmas parade for the aunts, however, there was no differentiation, and we all performed in some way, God help us, and as we were Katty's children we were all marvellous.

So the Christmas Day concert, while Father smiled and nodded and went on through the post – everyone's post; while this priest and that young nun peeped in and asked Reverend Mother (Aunt Mary) if they might listen awhile to all the wonderful talent of her nieces and nephews – until at last the Bishop of Limerick, in a lesser parlour waiting for Aunt Mary, was shown brilliantly in – and brilliant he was and looked, Edward Thomas O'Dwyer – so the concert went on. Broken only by applause, and by the episcopal entrance. Father, who loved Bishops and Princes of the Church – only imaginatively and with no experience of them – was delighted to have Aunt Mary place the deaf prelate beside him. He knew him well, and mounted him. Bishop O'Dwyer, who would allow none of his priests to hunt, was a great horseman.

So there they sat, shouting at each other. Bishop O'Dwyer shouted high and shrill anyway, and Father's only attack on the deaf – in this case useless – was to bellow.

And as they bellowed my sister Clare, persuaded by some gentle nuns near the piano, began to sing.

She sang "At the mid hour of night..." Father heard her when she began, and stopped shouting. The Bishop, glad enough no doubt to end an interchange he had nor head nor tail to, subsided into some note-taking, with a gold pencil on the back of an envelope. So I can hear the young, sad voice now, overcoming us all. She was already full contralto. She had had lessons from a local musician, but I think they meant nothing to Clare. I always thought, as I listened to her singing, that she was self-taught. She sang out of some knowledge that no Limerick teacher gave her. She sang, as few singers do, like a musician. She sang out of the centre of music. Often when we were young she sang ridiculous songs, but she never sang ridiculously. She gave musicianship to everything she sang. And that musicianship was her own – she did not learn it from any of her Limerick teachers.

"At the mid hour of night…". The young, rich voice, its purity seeming to contradict the great sorrow of the theme, still insisted that it knew what it sang. I think that Father, some Christmas card in his fidgety hand, could hardly bear the desolate and ghostly song – and yet he loved it.

Aunt Mary would break it up gently, patting Clare's shoulder, and asking her to play "The West's Awake" for Jack to sing, or "The Battle-Eve of the Irish Brigade."

"We must have something lively on Christmas Day," she would say. But Fan's tears fell faster for these songs than for "…when stars are weeping…" the long line of which bored her a little – whereas she was a patriot always before the first shout; and "Hurrah! Let England quake!" was very much her idea, even on Christmas Day and from her enclosed convent.

The Bishop rose and we with him, dropping all on one knee for his blessing – and a minute later one could watch him pacing down the garden, silky, silver hair blowing, pink hand cupping his good ear as he conversed with Aunt Mary, this Reverend Mother whom he admired extremely. His carriage horses champing, and even if the wind was cold he would linger with this nun – and *hear* what she said. An autocrat mostly disliked by his priests, a man of iron principle and courage as he was to prove in political troubles yet ahead, and one who expected to be listened to and obeyed, he often listened and often, I think, without knowing it obeyed when this young nun, his mere subaltern, spoke. It was known, and he always made clear, that he thought highly of her powers in office. But he was a man with an unexpected regard for the brains of women. He proved that in his long liking for the society of two unusually brainy nuns of Laurel Hill Convent, in Limerick. I was educated there, and I know how rarely intelligent were those two Latinists, Mother Lelia and Mother Thecla – and I know too how he liked to visit them, to tackle them about Latin, about the revival of Irish, about Irish history, and Ireland's future. His twanging, unpleasantly pitched voice was nevertheless clear and cultivated, and we could hear him from far off if it pleased him to walk into our garden classroom of an afternoon. Then he would take Horace out of Mother Thecla's hand, and singing out the Ode would turn mockingly on me or on Nellie Dundon or whomever, for a lightning scan. No use being scared; the thing was to make a stab at the lines – and he never mocked, always bent his good ear down attentively. Then after a few minutes he would slam the book shut, wave dismissal at us, and take Mother Thecla off into the garden in loud, learned argument, often talking Latin to her, to our deep edification.

Aunt Mary had no Latin, but she had wits and qualities he sought and too often missed among his fellow creatures. When he died his chaplain gave her, as a souvenir, a slim, shallow lacquered box – a useful and pleasant desk box, for pencils, sealing-wax, etc. And when she in her turn died, Fan gave it to me, because she knew that I agreed with Aunt Mary in admiring our difficult bishop, Edward Thomas of Limerick.

"Mary would like you to have it, pet. It was the

Bishop's collar-box."

"Collar-box, Fan?"

"Always, I believe, he kept his collars in it."

"But, Fan – he couldn't! Look at it! It's a pencil box."

"Are you going to contradict me about what the Bishop's Chaplain said? Anyway, a bishop's collars are very small – "

The Bishop's collar-box is still among the chattels on my desk, and is always known as Fan christened it. And it reminds me from time to time of two admirable and very holy people, who admired each other in holiness.

Auntie Mick watched them in the garden, as I did.

"You'd wonder how Mary puts up with all that screeching," she said.

"She's very fond of the Bishop," said Fan.

"'Tis as well," said Auntie Mick. "Anyway, Tom, that beautiful pair of bays are getting their death waiting for him. You should never sell blood animals to the Bishop. His coachman, Murnane, is a holy disgrace, Mick tells me!"

Father laughed.

"And God bless Mick! That stepping pair outside are still about the best in the country, Anne – after two years in Murnane's charge!"

Soon Auntie Mick would leave, having sipped a glass of port, eaten several chocolates and two very large crystallised fruits – all under pressure – and having run a quick eye over as many as possible of the Christmas cards, although Father enjoyed tricking her about them. She had brought no presents to the Convent – which everyone felt was as well, because her presents to us had been of their usual embarrassing meanness. But to Aunt Mary, embracing her at departure she said, ironically smiling at the candy boxes and fruit baskets which we had brought and were rapidly stripping – "I brought no worldly offerings, Mary, having a true respect for holy poverty. But I hope my flowers in the Crib will speak for me – "

Her flower-pots, chrysanthemums, cyclamens, brought by her gardener on Christmas Eve, were indeed wonderful; but they were only lent, and the convent had plenty of its own. And anyway, she always gave the most and the pick of her greenhouses to the Jesuits. We all knew this but, in the presence of nuns who were not of the family, none of us winked at each other. However when she went on: "In any case, Mick as you know will be generous as always to the convent at New Year..." Father did wink, very neatly, at Fan, who got the giggles. However they were behind Auntie Mick, who made a stately exit, and was escorted from the parlour and down the garden by some anxiously polite young nun.

With her gone and the Bishop, the pace of feast-day quickened in the parlour. Blushing novices slipped in to wish happy Christmas to Reverend Mother's "lovely family", and with any luck to hear May, the eldest of us, sing "The Snowy-Breasted Pearl", looking the while so like the heroine of her song; or Nance recite "O'Rourke's Request" brilliantly; or Father Thornhill, our handsome, heavy cousin, oblige with a great long roar of "Dark Rosaleen" (I also had to make a fair fool of myself, for I was an accomplished reciter, and I think, looking back, that unless someone had upset me beforehand, I enjoyed my own ghastly performances – of "Only Daisies", or something). Anyway I do believe those nuns enjoyed us all; the five boys were good at entertainment; they could sing – except Michael; they could do little bits from school plays; Tom could recite "Eugene Aram"; they could conjure; Father could juggle oranges or apples – and he could sing.

But so could some of the vain, shy, visiting curates – and so could Sister Bernardine. Thus, the programme was crowded. However, enraptured or not, people talked and moved about through performances – and ate Turkish delight too if it suited them, and drank port. So the strain was light.

And Aunt Mary, Reverend Mother, governed all.

When one recalls how greatly she was adored through her religious life, in her various offices and finally as Reverend Mother, it is interesting to consider the calm of her government. On such a day of licence in the parlour as Christmas Day, through which almost all her nuns flowed and various priests, and polite laymen too such as the convent doctor or dentist, called to pay respects, one can consider her concealed character. She was without pomp, and no one would ever know from watching her actions or hearing her observations within the group that she was head man, so to speak. She rarely sat down; she always seemed restless and young; she had no intellectual pretensions whatever, and she made no especial outward cult of edification or of piety; and as I came to know as I grew up, she could take a joke against the Church as amusedly as any subtle Monsignor. Also as I came to observe, she had, not pure theology, but all the essential arguments of moral theology at her finger-tips. This makes one wonder – in one who had been a village girl at a village school, and with only two years at a small convent boarding-school to train her for the very difficult life she was to choose and to command.

I suppose that not only wisdom, but the more precise thing, knowledge comes to the gifted out of the occasions that exact it. It seems a close-cut way; I do not understand how the timing works. But it must be at least that repetition of experiences which call for knowledge of human life, the human heart and the various defeating puzzles of human nature can teach that knowledge almost in shorthand to the innocent – the intelligent innocent.

Aunt Mary had this luck, this ease of acquisition. Not always. I have seen her break down, and be worldly, and even silly. But that was before circumstances which her nun's career had made difficult for her to grasp. All experience however that could be contained within a convent and which related to its rules and vows – all that I think she understood as if by special vocation.

AUNT HICKEY

Aunt Hickey, whose born name was Anne O'Brien, was Father's only sister. She was twenty years old and engaged to be married when he was born in the early 1850s. An explanation for the long gap between Father and his two brothers and one sister may be a succession of deaths of small children in between. The times were bad; famine and disease were commonplace. It is probable that Father's mother lost many children, and that he owed his survival to the relative prosperity, decency and hope of Grandfather's optimistic beginnings in Limerick city – after his eviction in the late 1840s.

When we were being born Aunt Hickey's children were marrying and becoming engaged. She may have been already a grandmother, I think, before our father's eldest child was born.

She had married a very handsome, irritable and slight man called John Hickey who dealt, like father, in bloodstock horses, and who lived in Mespil Road in Dublin, in the house and large paddock now occupied by Iris Kellett and her riding school.

The Hickeys lived handsomely. Everything they wore came from Switzer's or houses of that level. Everything they ate or drank came from Findlater or Leverett and Frye. Uncle Hickey was an exacting and peppery man. If luncheon was for one o'clock, then woe betide whoever caused delay or hold-up. If his carving knives were not in perfect form, then woe again to everybody. I remember being amused once at home when he was our guest, but of course had to carve – tolerating no other carving. Our good Lizzie had placed the dishes, and stood at his left hand waiting to take the plates. But she had grown dreamy. He sat staring at her a minute and then, in a fury, banged on the silver dish cover with his carving fork. She had forgotten to lift the great affair. I remember how our usually imperturbable Lizzie jumped to snatch it off. He was that kind of fusspot. Handsome and all as he was I never liked him.

Aunt Hickey wore sable stoles and sealskin jackets. She had always perfect umbrellas and muffs, and she wore chains and jewels, and had a lovely watch pinned with diamonds to her breast. Her clothes were silky and discreet; she exhaled Dublin worldliness.

She was tall and not fat, but strong-looking. She had coal-black hair, and curiously for Munster her eyes were hazel to brown. Their colour varied, but was never blue or grey.

I must describe Aunt Hickey's mouth. It was one of the most remarkably expressive mouths I have ever observed in my life, and I think that details observed and retained are usually of greater interest than broad impressions. Certainly Aunt Hickey never recurs to my memory but that I see that astonishing and hyper-civilised movement of smile across her upper lip. This slow, cut-out curving of the lip, which was supported by a strong line of the lower mouth and which swept across splendid, large teeth, might have been described as sardonic, but it was so unusual and beautiful and so like the incoming turn of a wave of the sea that I always watched for it in sheer pleasure, indifferent to what it expressed, held by its motion of power and beauty.

If Father had not worn a clipped moustache, he might well have had something of this remarkable chiselled curve to show in his smile, and he also had beautiful teeth, whiter and smaller than Aunt Hickey's. But the best-looking of the latter's children, her daughter Kitty who married the great rugby international, Louis Magee, inherited from her mother this truly remarkable and sensitive curve of the upper lip. Kitty was beautiful, with a tender, good-humoured, white-skinned beauty which her dark-skinned mother missed – but she reproduced the fascinating, hyper-expressive mouth which I have tried to describe, and which in both faces was a perpetual subject of wonder and entertainment to me.

Aunt Hickey was not sentimental. All the Thornhills were, and so was Father, whose temperament was curiously sympathetic to that of his "in-laws".

I remember with amusement this:

We were in the Presentation Parlour. Aunt Hickey who was staying with us was making a state call on the nuns, and two or three of us young ones had been turned on, as pages more or less, to accompany her.

I imagine that Aunt Mary admired Aunt Hickey, even respected the worldly aplomb of the much older woman, with all her Dublin appurtenances and ideas. (Aunt Hickey was as extravagant and generous as Auntie Mick was mean – and her presents to us and all her own equipment gave off the aroma of wealth.) I think that Fan found her a bit puzzling perhaps, and I'd take a fair guess that to Aunt Annie she was unsympathetic, just someone to be formal with.

To a child she certainly was not easy to know, and for all her open-handedness and indeed good humour she seemed too grown up, perhaps just too old, to be understandable. Yet I liked to watch her mouth, as I have said, and to study her jewels and fine equipment.

I have veered from my story.

This day in the Parlour some young nun, invited to sing, had obliged with a ballad called "Rory Darling". This was a great favourite of Fan's, for it told the sad story of an eviction "...we must leave the little cabin that we built in days of yore..." and Fan liked nothing better than to get herself thoroughly upset over the Famine and the Land War.

When Sister Mary Teresa had finished this sad little story, Fan, enormous check handkerchief in hand, was drying her sweet blue eyes and polishing her glasses. But she felt that perhaps the choice of song was a little awkward, since Aunt Hickey's parents had suffered eviction in her girlhood, and she had had to "leave the little cabin...etc." So timidly she had laid her hand on one of Aunt Hickey's beautifully gloved ones.

"Ah, Anne," she said. "She shouldn't have sung that. I can well imagine the sad memories it brings back – " Aunt Hickey laughed, and patted the kind hand.

"Have sense, Fan," said she. "If ever there was a fortunate eviction wasn't it my father's ?"

She was right. But right or wrong, I think that Aunt Hickey can never have been the girl to linger around the "little cabin". She would have taken off for the large world, surely, had her father not been compelled to.

She married a severe and arrogant Dubliner; Uncle Hickey was very handsome, slim and lively, always very well dressed; an opinionated and wilful kind of man, but of no great intelligence. He had to have his own way in all unimportant things, and must have been lacking in humour.

We used to be told of him that if a tram conductor said "O'Connell Bridge" when he, Uncle Hickey, had asked for Carlisle Bridge, or said O'Connell Street when the request had been for Sackville Street, he would refuse his fare and descend from the tram. He could weep sometimes over "our great little Queen", and work himself into violent defence of the English nobles or whatever they were who governed Ireland from Dublin Castle. What can have been the matter with an ordinary Irish horse dealer, to have him going on like that? Certainly he made most of his money out of the ascendancy, but so did Father, and although he was never rude about his customers, he never spoke as other than an ordinary troubled Irishman, who had put his faith in Parnell, and afterwards, because of their loyalty to Parnell, continued to trust the John Redmond Home Rule Party.

I think Aunt Hickey cared not at all for politics – though I believe she may have smiled that beautiful sardonic smile of hers sometimes at the loyalist absurdities of her husband. Be that as it may, their children – being born in the 1870s and 1880s, five daughters and one son – were brought up in detachment from the troubles of their day, and in acceptance of the standards of middle-class success. The girls went to convents in England, I cannot imagine why; and the one son Jack – I do not know where he learnt his little Latin and no Greek – perhaps at Belvedere. But schooling and lesson books never stayed the Hickeys' interest; they were not in the most elementary sense for scholarship, nor did their parents expect them so to be.

When I was a child they were all either married or engaged, or anyhow out on the tides of the Dublin world, swimming away – with children and carriages and accounts at Switzer's.

But there is a piece of fun which I am trying to reach through all this build-up. Father was fond of his

Dublin sister and her family, and took a great interest in them, their marriages and babies, and Jack Hickey's triumphs of horsemanship, at the Horse Show, and with the Kildares, and the Ward Union Point-to-Point, and all. But he was also very fond indeed of his own children; and when we were growing up we were for the most part very good at our lessons, and good examinees. We all went in for winning exhibitions and prizes awarded by the Intermediate Board of Education every summer. The results of these June examinations were published in September – and almost always in the lists some one of Father's children had really distinguished his or herself. This was wine to Father – he absolutely adored to have any child of his do well in anything – though no one gentler or more considerate of you if you failed, or half-failed.

Anyhow, when Father had the Intermediate Board results all printed out in the *Irish Times* on a September day, there was no holding him. Some of us, perhaps three or four of us, would have done very well, with exhibitions or prizes – but every year our sister Nance walked off with the All-Ireland Bronze Medal for English Composition. Higher than this you could not go, within the system – and Father was not to be held.

For some reason, he always had to telephone the Hickeys of Mespil Road about these Intermediate results. People less likely to be interested than that ageing pair, who, nor whose children, had ever sat for an examination in their lives, it would be hard to imagine.

But Father loved telephoning, and he loved good news.

So after tea he'd get 39 Mespil Road on the line. He always roared into the instrument – "I'm speaking to Dublin, dammit!" – and so he roared away at Uncle

Hickey. Newspaper in hand, he read out all our triumphs of scholarship.

"Splendid, Tom, splendid!"

"But listen to this, about Nance! Nance has won the Bronze Medal of All-Ireland for English Composition! All Ireland, man!"

"Great, Tom – that Nancy is a great little girl. There's no doubt she'll be out *on top* next time!"

"What I'm telling you is that she *is* out on top! She has beaten everyone of her age in Ireland! She has the Bronze Medal! The top prize!"

"Yes – grand, Tom, grand. Tell her from me that she's bound to be out on top next time!"

"She's out on top this time, man!"

"Yes – there's no doubt – she'll manage it next time! Right out on top! You'll see, Tom – I'm sure of it."

Father would leave the telephone, drenched in sweat and rage. But then he would soothe himself by ringing Fermoy, and telling Aunt Annie all about the Bronze Medal.

Uncle Hickey was a peculiar man, because for all his loyalty to the Crown and the Castle he fell under the spell of Father Mathew, and on some dramatic evening took the life Abstinence Pledge from the great apostle of Temperance, on the steps of the Adam and Eve Church. That pledge taken became an absolute, and although no one was grudged whatever kind of liquid refreshment they required in his house – Aunt Hickey would not in any case have tolerated prohibitions of any kind – the uncle himself was a ramrod of abstinence for all his days after he took that pledge. It seems that once when he was gravely ill and the doctors judged some drops of brandy advisable to pull him through a crisis, Aunt Hickey got up to some dodgery and sent the prescribed alcohol down his throat – and on confession afterwards was never forgiven. According to his enraged protest he would rather have died than break the pledge he gave to Father Mathew.

He lived to be very old, and I do not know if the trick was ever pulled on him again in any of his last illnesses, but he would certainly have been on the watch. He did not forgive Aunt Hickey for saving his life.

He had one great grief, the death in her early married life of his beautiful eldest daughter, Molly. The marriage had not been happy, and it seems that Uncle Hickey was haunted by guilt for his own promotion of it, for worldly reasons. Anyhow he went through a long life unable to forget it, and in moments of weariness or loneliness would be heard muttering about it in self-recrimination. Also as a very old man he had to bear the death in his thirty-third year of his only son.

It is hard to understand why Jack Hickey died as and when he did. He lived only for physical fitness, for hunting, polo-playing and show-jumping. In all of these he excelled, and to look at he was the very expression of horsey style and perfection in the male. Except for a perhaps too Roman nose he was superbly handsome; graceful, slim, unassuming and sweetly mannered – quite without intellect, but with great charm and modesty, he went through life indolently, extravagantly and having his fun, possibly quite serious fun, among the ladies. Not among the girls. Jack Hickey liked sophisticated women – women much wittier and more worldly-wise than he.

And then while still temperamentally no more than a boy he had some kind of stroke, and in two days was dead.

It was a savage blow to the two aged parents, for he was their last-born and hardly-hoped-for when he came – and their only son. Both must have been over eighty at that time; and I think it broke up Uncle Hickey completely – that, and the selling, which had to follow, of their beloved 39 Mespil Road. I think he became gently senile in the following years, and did not live long. For all he knew, poor old man, he may have broken Father Mathew's pledge, unwillingly, before the end. But I hope not.

Aunt Hickey was of harder stuff than her husband, and, her house taken from her – that house which she ruled with warmth, hospitality and style – she was yet to live a long time, authoritatively and philosophically, in the houses of her daughters, and at last in a nursing home.

But my last picture of her is still in Mespil Road, in 1918 – not long after the death of her son Jack. She was sitting in her sort of large greenhouse-room, with her daughter Dolly, and they were examining dusty bills off an old bill-hook. They had no money at all now, having always spent everything as it came. They were, I could see, in fair perplexity.

They had a nice old parrot, very old. And he came down off his ring and settled on Aunt Hickey's shoulder, lovingly.

"Damn Switzer's," he said to her.

She leant back and kissed him, and for the last time I saw the wonderful wave-of-the-sea smile across her proud old mouth.

"God bless you, Sam," she said to the parrot.

AUNTIE MICK

Auntie Mick, passing in and out of the Parlour infrequently, seemed there perhaps only a stiff, tall nobody. A nobody, that is, in relation to that place, where sensibility decided all. A nobody because, although no one who frequented the Parlour, from Aunt Fan to Sister Lucy to our baby brother Gerard, would have thought thus, she represented judgement and not for a moment feeling. And she stood also in the "in-law" relationship – the only family visitor to Mary and Fan who was related in law alone. For Father was not only our father, but from long ago, as Katty's husband, their beloved brother; and Aunt Hickey was Father's sister, however much her Dublin grandeurs might confuse or annoy. But Auntie Mick was only the wife, the childless wife, of Father's silly old brother. She was a stranger, and had mean turns of speech.

But a nobody outside of the Presentation Parlour she was not.

Her marriage to Uncle Mick took place late in his fifties, at a guess, and when she very likely was approaching forty; and their life together, although orthodox and even sometimes marked by eccentricities of devotion, was inharmonious. And whereas it may have been sad it had mostly the appearance of a comic life. Auntie Mick would not have liked to think that she and her husband made such an impression; but Uncle Mick was a comic character, quite stupendously one; he was a Dickensian oddity, unmanageably baroque and obstinately foolish. And it is possible that she, who had been a proud and independent schoolteacher, may even have had to be wily in getting the amiable and talkative scatterbrain, our uncle, to the point and to the altar. That one cannot know. And what she wanted with him one might wonder until, coming to understand her genius for *grande dame* style, one saw his usefulness. Moreover, there may even have been a glitter of fact in the sentimental story which family surmise built in behind the curious marriage.

"So you are liking *The Mill on the Floss*?"

We were sitting in a curved window in the inner of the two large drawing-rooms of Shannon View. There was a meagre tea-tray on a lovely little table beside us – some biscuits and stale end of Madeira cake, but the teapot was an exquisite piece of silver, and our cups enchanted me. I do not know their name, even now; they were not precious. Auntie Mick had a china room full of precious cups and dishes, but when she asked me to tea we always had this white porcelain; bright blue band below the golden lip, little tiny golden studs outlining the bright blue. I remember those cups still, with an anxious kind of love.

Auntie Mick made me anxious; I think now that she did so because she was unkind and mean; but then I was not sure of anything, and such simple badnesses may not have seemed possible to me, because I liked her and I liked the things she told me and the books she lent me.

"If you're interested in *The Mill on the Floss* I'll tell you about George Eliot."

And she did. She told me what she knew, and it was accurate, about the childhood, youth and young womanhood of Mary Ann Evans, and roused in me much of what was her own passionate feeling for that young and formidable bluestocking. Spread over readings, she told me of the great novels I would read later, of the worldly success and the mastery. Naturally, I heard nothing of G. H. Lewes; but I remember that she surprised me one afternoon by saying of her heroine:

"She married, when she was sixty, a young admirer, Mr Cross. That was foolish. She died the same year."

Although my tea-time conversations with Auntie Mick were interesting, they were a cause of embarrassment too. She lived in a splendid Georgian house, surrounded by beautiful gardens and meadows, about three miles outside Limerick. It was the house to which Father should have brought Mother, and where we should all have grown up, but somehow his half-dotty elder brother decided to live there when the firm bought the place, took his wife there to express her histrionic self, while he indulged his connoisseur tastes in spaciousness – and we stayed to be born in Grandfather's original brick villa. Absurd arrangement – for from Grandfather's death onwards Father was the only money-spinner, the only horse-flesh expert and the only worker in the partnership; but the elder brother, with his flair for furniture and bibelots and his naturally *grande dame* wife – to the manner gifted, not born – took themselves happily off to the big house, which was made for family life, and not for sterile fiddle-faddling.

But we used to drive in pony-traps, or ride donkeys out to Shannon View when we felt inclined, and pass long, happy days there. We were not very hospitably received, upstairs; but in the vast kitchen regions there were angels – Mrs Clancy, and Amelia and Josie and Mrs Moriarty, the hen-woman; and Staunton, and the Mearas, Tom and Pat, and old Crowe. All these, in and out, loved us, and let us run mad – through dairy and saddle-room and kitchen garden, and wherever we chose. And because Auntie Mick was a great committee woman and public servant, half her time she was away with her high-stepping cob and her nervous groom, and did not know until late afternoon that Tom's dislikeable brood were all over her estate.

The word 'dislikeable' points my difficulty about Auntie Mick. It was a point of honour in our family to be disliked by her. My eldest brother Jack she expressly loathed, and that was his high feather; another totally disliked was my triumphant sister Nancy; these two were magnificent in confronting her with flat lies – about missing apples, broken raspberry canes, what you will. They were wonderful cold liars. No evidence flustered them. And they were lying only to her. They knew that we all, standing round, knew the facts and were with them, in admiring silence. They were shields and guardians of us all. And they truly did keep that tyrant in some measure in her place. We used to wonder why then. Now I understand that their power, those gallant, cheeky ones, was not theirs but simply their father's. I understand that for those latter years when *we* children knew the grandeurs of Shannon View Father was paying for their upkeep.

My quarry here, however, is not the painful economic situation of my proud aunt-in-law – but only her isolated person. And isolated is a good word for the character of Auntie Mick. To be liked by her when one was a child was to be under some shadow with the other children, and in doubt oneself. And she did like me. She liked Tom also, a brother two years older than me; and as he was a strong and original character this consoled me a little for the embarrassment of her favour. It was he or I – never both – who was usually sent for to have tea with her. And the others mocked as we walked obediently to the house.

But – she was a natural educator. She bought and understood books; she read and, in her sphere, took part in public affairs. So having tea with her was not dull. She was a shrewd director of a child's mind, and she showed me how to read, and made me read beyond my age, and with zest. I owe her much of what I might prefer to call my self-education. She made me read Milton and Pope, for instance, when I was thirteen-fourteen, and she told me much about their lives, and their respective places in history and literature. She gave me Dr Johnson's *Lives of the Poets* to read, and examined me on them closely. And if she did make me toil through *Evangeline* and *Miles Standish*, God help me, she also lent me Macaulay's *Essays* and made me read Byron.

I never forgot what she said one day about the Brontës: "They were held to be unhappy women, and they did die young, all of them. But I think they were happy children and that is a lot."

When I have reflected on that true comment, I have been puzzled that it was given to me by a woman who was mean and cruel to children. Auntie Mick was a mix-up, no doubt – but for the most part, when all charitable allowances are made, she was mean and cruel in her life, and cruel to children.

I admired her appearance. She was tall and she dressed well, very correctly, with the right kind of jewellery, with excellent umbrellas, toques and gloves. She was self-indulgent in these things, I imagine, and she almost vocally grudged good quality anything to everyone but herself. The only photograph which has survived of her insults her subtle, long face. There was a snapshot of her in her rose garden – in garden hat and gloves, with basket and clippers – very slender, very *grande dame*, which really did express her cold grace. But it is lost. The official photograph insults her.

She wore light, small capes, and a silver châtelaine at her slim and silver-belted waist, and rings that slipped loosely on her bony fingers. She gardened well, and knew every rose that opened for her. She had wonderful gardens, and a rose garden which she guarded like the mean tiger she was. She knew about trees and shrubs; she could identify birds. She was widely and richly informative – but information was the only thing she found it easy to part with. She was in fact mean; and in our family that was a freakish thing to be.

It was all the more freakish to be mean and married to Uncle Mick. That indeed made a calamitous and comic situation.

Uncle Mick was possibly as unintelligent as Auntie Mick was intelligent; he was also as generous and warm-hearted as she was grudging and cold. What Uncle Mick was in manhood I cannot imagine; in my time he was an old man, uncomfortably married to a contemptuous wife; a foolish and eccentric man, crazily generous, amiable and obstinate, and with an exuberant, untrained flair for certain kinds of bibelots and antique objects. He was indeed a mad collector – and I think that in certain fields of this interest he had an innocent good taste, which is one kind of knowledge. Anyhow, from auctions of china, of furniture, of pictures, he could not be held; and Shannon View, the large country house in which he lived, childless, with his sardonic wife, was crammed with his random buyings.

Some of them lovely.

Uncle Mick had, I think, an uneducated or self-educated judgement for certain kinds of pictures. Arrangements in frames which in their especial kind were good he tended to buy. Needlework pictures, pictures in silk, Chinese silk strips, early nineteenth-century steel engravings in lovely pale gilt frames – these crowded the walls of Shannon View. He bought delicate china too, and Persian saddle-bags, and Persian carpets. On furniture he was not especially original or good, though he had some good mahogany. I remember his beautiful sideboard and wine cooler. And he bought good silver.

Meantime he posed – disastrously for our family fortunes – as an impeccable judge of horseflesh. Father always said that Uncle Mick was ruinously bad in horse buying. He even went so far as to say that his elder brother and senior partner was in fact afraid of horses, and did not understand them at all. Since Father's expertise on them was, like his father's, renowned throughout Ireland, the lack of this talent in Uncle Mick need not have mattered, were it not that their horse-breeding business was a partnership, and that Uncle Mick as senior partner had full purchasing freedom. Seemingly he was forever buying useless old knackers of horses at extravagant prices – which Father had to dispose of at loss and quickly, so as not to lower the high tradition of his stables.

Meantime, Uncle Mick could buy china and bibelots with success, so it is a pity for all of us that he did not transfer himself to the old furniture trade – he *was* afraid of horses.

I do not know when he married Anne Liddy – Auntie Mick – or why. Father had another brother John, who lived abroad and had been dead long before I was born, I think. This Uncle Johnny was handsome indeed, if the small portrait still extant is to be counted on. He looked after the English and

European end of our grandfather's business – and that was extensive, for we mounted cavalry officers in many countries, sold hunters to all the great M.F.H.s. and matched carriage horses for the nobility everywhere. We mounted Elizabeth of Austria, for instance – and Uncle Mick was not to be stopped when he got on to the subject of the Empress. It seems he knew her like the back of his hand! And when she came to hunt in Ireland, he was put in charge of her string of hunters, according to himself. But I do not believe that Grandfather would have allowed that. Anyway, there were signed drawings of her all about Shannon View. But Uncle Johnny was the man in charge of all that foreign connection – and it used to be said in the family that on one of his visits home he met the severe and ambitious Miss Anne Liddy, and gave her to understand that he was in love with her. Be that as it may, she married not him but his foolish elder brother. He, Johnny, married a French ballerina or music-hall artist, and died young abroad, of tuberculosis –

All that before my time. But assuredly Auntie Mick would occasionally speak to us in hushed and admiring tones of our dead Uncle Johnny. And I believe that she likely did have some kind of light within her dark heart for him. Life in the large world with him would have suited her intelligence and her ambitions, and had she lived in London she would have been a pioneer and militant suffragette, I have no doubt. For she did believe in the powers and rights of women; she believed in the application of brains to current problems, and she was an efficient and formidable committee woman.

Poor Law Guardian work, children's fosterage and boarding-out committees, Cottage Gardens committees and so on – they were all she could get her teeth into in Limerick. But she worked at them, and made others work.

She had, outside her inner ring of domestic meanness and suspiciousness, a hard sense of justice and a cool vision that became her well, and emphasised her real intelligence. Indeed, in all that did not press too close against herself, in all that was not family life, her own family life, Auntie Mick could judge and measure well, could be fair, and could be humorous.

There were days when it was her business to drive about and visit certain boarded-out workhouse children round her bailiwick, and some of us might go with her on these trips. She was lively and enjoyable then – informative about trees or birds or ruined castles as they passed. And even carefully amusing about the cottages and cottage women we visited.

It is all very old hat now, but as social effort went in Auntie Mick's time this housing of poor little workhouse bastards in country places with family groups was not a bad idea. We did not know that the boarded-out were bastard, need I say, and we were made to come into each cottage and fraternise with the children while Auntie Mick went through her questionnaire with the woman of the house. The latter was usually nervous, I used to notice, even when most affable – and who would blame her who could see my aunt's cool eyes appraising everything in sight and all the humble domestic arrangements? This it was her duty to do, as Poor Law Guardian – and I admit she managed to do it with a certain humour and ease. But it cannot have been a comfortable half-hour for the visited – and I for one could not make any kind of social progress with the gaping, overawed children in the cottages. Some of them terrified me indeed, I remember. But none of them had any use for me, or I for them. One was as glad to get back into the pony trap as they were to see one out the door.

Still, on those expeditions I got to know my socially-conscienced aunt, and indeed, in some wonder, to admire her. And the drives through the sweet lanes were lovely – especially if we were on inspection of Cottage Gardens – when Auntie, a real gardener, was very much interested and in earnest with her encouragement, advice and note-taking – or if we were sampling soda bread. That, the series of hot slices eagerly presented, could be agreeable to the point of surfeit.

This aunt never made any pretences or false gestures; she was as simple as anyone else about her simple origins – and indeed to have been otherwise would have struck her as totally ridiculous. But in her social work her friends were often local baronets and peeresses, and she was, as it happened, in appearance and manner more than a match for any of them, although now and then, very oddly – say in anger with a gardener or a maidservant – she might betray a shocking kind of ill-breeding in the cruelty of her face and speech. Yet her closest friend in long years was probably Lady Emly, an English aristocrat who was the second wife of that interesting Viscount Emly of Tervoe who was a contemporary at Oxford with Newman and Aubrey de Vere, and a convert to Catholicism with them in the Oxford Movement. Auntie Mick could narrate the Oxford Movement quite lucidly to a child, and told me much about Newman. And I think if she was lastingly fond of anyone outside the family it was Lady Emly. But affection she was poor in, either as giver or receiver. And alas one could always see why.

Simply she was mean, poor woman. She must have been greedy too, because it was always clear that the best of everything was good enough for her, though no one else was allowed to claim it.

Her immense kitchen garden was beautifully gardened, no expense or labour spared; and she loved to walk through to it from her equally beautiful rose garden, and to pace its walks in contemplation. She liked very much too to catch some of us thieving there – as often she did – among the raspberry canes or up the apple trees. I remember three or four of us throwing ourselves flat between asparagus hedges once when we saw her afar off. But we did not escape, need I say? We had to rise in humiliation and march before her to the house, lashed all the way by her contemptuous and, in that moment, bitterly vulgar tongue.

I have wondered sometimes what she did with all the fruits of her great garden? For she truly grudged them even to her own dining-table, if we were present – let alone to any other. Did she sell them ? She liked to flatter the Jesuits with gifts – and perhaps she made offerings to the nuns at the workhouse, or to her committee friends. Anyhow, we were given as nearly nothing from that garden as makes no matter – and though we thieved with fair skill, to carry off one rose from any tree of Auntie Mick's was as frightening an experience as it was in *Beauty and the Beast*. As frightening, but no fairy tale.

What harm but poor Uncle Mick was forever trying to lavish the gifts of his own estate on us.

"I'm going to send in a load of those roses to Boru House," he'd say, loudly, to keep his courage up. Or "I'm having a basket of strawberries picked for the children in the morning, Anne!"

The look she would give him! He must have got into fearful trouble time and time again. But when he got off the leash, in the town, he could make up for these frustrations. On Saturdays he used to bring us what he called "the fairings" – whatever rich fruits were in season, and beautiful boxes of chocolates and candies too. He called us by an extraordinary collective word, from the Irish. "Where are the Kinnemackonies ?" he'd shout. "I've brought the fairings!"

Poor old man – all smiles and happy, released mischief. He cannot have had much of a private life. It is recorded in the family – I do not remember this – that in Mother's time, when we were asked out to Shannon View for the afternoon, Mother always quite shamelessly brought cakes and cream and fruit – and these were coolly accepted, but grudgingly put on the tea-table by Auntie Mick.

An unhappy temperament – because in some directions so expressively intelligent and just.

She was censorious of much, being so literate. I remember her coming into our house one day, showing May a book that she had lent her – a library book – and throwing it on the fire.

"That is the only right place for that novel, child," she said. I do not think she offered to pay the cost at the lending library. But she looked wonderfully amused and arrogant as she flung the book in the fire, and I have not forgotten the laugh with which she did it. I think the novel was called *The Dop Doctor.*

DEPARTURES

Auntie Mick was the first of the aunts to take off into the dark, or into perpetual light, whichever it is.

I know a great deal about her death and its ambience, for it took place – slowly, slowly – during the Easter vacation of 1918. I was down from the university and idling round, and so my young brother Eric and I – he was about eighteen – were put more or less in charge of the sad and comic goings-on at St John's Villas.

I can imagine no death as a farcical subject – and Auntie Mick's was real, cruel death, like any other; inexorable and awful. But her husband, always comic, was in his last years an abandoned eccentric; and in senile distraction he turned all the circumstances beyond the little death room into rare farce.

Circumstances had changed pathetically for Auntie Mick in what were to be the last twenty months of her life.

Our father had died in June 1916, and whatever were the complicated ins-and-outs of his support of the glories of Shannon View, during that summer lawyers and bankers called a stop to them. The place was sold, and the spoilt old pair came to live on the edge of the town, in a mean little brick villa, a couple of stone throws from our house. No garden, only a concrete yard and a miserable patch in front, beside a dusty road; no roses, no greenhouses, no stables, no stepping thoroughbreds, no servants outdoor or indoor. A few, a very few of the precious engravings and bibelots, a Persian rug or two, some of the smallest pieces of the highly cherished furniture. None of these things seemed to settle down in the little jerry-built house – but Uncle and Auntie Mick had to do so. And did it with surprising grace.

She still had her personal elegance, her châtelaine and her little capes; she had too her coolness, her habit of insolence and reserve. He, always a blustery, talkative, gregarious fellow and a sly tippler, now no doubt found it easier to pursue his habits of conviviality than it had been in the days of cut-off state, when Auntie Mick had allowed no casual hospitality and kept all decanters securely under her private lock and key.

So they were placed in St John's Villas, and not as unhappily as might have been expected. I presume they were very poor. Her committee days were over; Lady Emly was dead, and the Great War and Easter 1916 had broken up all the old routines. People and ideas of her heyday were scattered, and her health was failing. She was tired once she left Shannon View. But she read newspapers, and novels – burning the latter when she thought it advisable. She often came and sat by the fire in our house, or in the garden; she ate well if she stayed to dinner, and she still liked very much, while protesting, to eat any delicacies which *she* had not provided. She said many prayers at this time, and read much in her Missal and in Lives of the Saints. She remained an interesting and informative talker. But she just was tired. Early in 1918 she took greatly to her bed, and during Lent it was recognised that she was deep into her last illness. What it was I do not know, or what her age.

When I came down on vacation during Passion week I went to see her, and was shocked by her wasted body, and darkened skin. She was pleased to see me, said she had been waiting for me and asked me to hand her a little box from her dressing-table. Out of this her twisted hand took a gold chain and locket that I had often seen her wear. They were very beautiful, very heavy. She put them into my hands.

"I want you to have them," she said. "Keep them. You're too young for them now, but wear them when you are a famous writer."

I had been a favourite – and this was favouritism indeed. And God alone knows where they are now, that locket and chain – for I lost them long before I could call myself any kind of writer, good or bad. The next day she went into a coma, out of which the doctor told us she would not return, and that she must be regarded now as at the end of her life.

Uncle Mick cried and cried a very great deal, but then he accepted the fact – and the farce began.

When on Palm Sunday the doctor reported that the heart and pulse of the lost, still figure on the bed were still strong, and that he could not say how few or many days death would take at its conclusive work, Uncle Mick began to worry.

Holy Week would be a very awkward week for a funeral. People would not be reading the papers much, or in the country places getting them at all – and there would be no papers on Good Friday. And if Auntie Mick died on or just before Good Friday she would probably have to be buried in haste on Saturday, on account of the great Church feast of Easter. But if she died on Saturday or Sunday it might be worse, because over the holidays there would be no local papers – and no one at all would be able to attend her funeral on Tuesday.

Now Anne – "I always called her Anne and she always called me Mick," he would keep wailing – Anne was to have such a monster and thronged and grief-stricken funeral as Limerick had never seen or imagined. There must be no doubt or mistake about that. And here she was in an immeasurable coma at the beginning of the most awkward week of the year, if one is planning funerals. What to do?

The old man worked himself into an obsession with the problem.

All the Limerick papers appear in the late afternoon or evening, and usually do not reach country places until the next day. There are none on Sunday, and of course none on Good Friday.

He asked me, he asked everyone what was the procedure about obituary notices. I told him that from our side there was none, that when Auntie died we would ring the local papers and tell them to print the customary announcement of death – and that was all. He seemed deeply dissatisfied with this. He kept going upstairs to look at her where she lay, a quiet Blue Nun in charge of her – then would come down wailing her praises – poor foolish chant: "She was an extraordinary woman! She had an extraordinary career, an extraordinary career! Wait till I tell you! She was born in this parish, she was baptised and confirmed in this parish, she taught in this parish, she was married in this parish, she died in this parish, and she'll be buried in this parish! An extraordinary career!" He cried out this poor litany to every comer. One had to say sometimes – "Hush, Uncle, she *hasn't* died." "She has, she has! She died in the parish!" And "I always called her Anne and she always called me Mick." Eric and I often got bad giggles.

But one evening we arrived into the little house to

find him standing in the small dining-room with, seated at the table, pencils and pads before them, four young men. Reporters from the *Limerick Chronicle*, the *Limerick Leader*, the *Munster News* and the *Evening Echo*. They told us who they were, and they looked both amused and embarrassed. We asked them how on earth? "Your uncle sent for us," they said. How he had arranged that we never found out; but there he had them, and he was engaged in dictating to them the obituary of his still living wife.

"Take it down as I say, young men...a lady of the highest virtue and generosity, renowned in city and country for her works of charity, and for her great piety. Her price was above rubies to us all – above rubies, mind you! Have you got that?" He seemed very proud of his piece of prose, and paused to relight his cigar, looking almost happy. "She had an extraordinary career – she was born in the parish, she was..."

"Not that, Uncle."

Eric and I managed somehow to break it up. Anyway, he must have been dictating for some time, as he seemed satisfied; and I think the journalists had already had the "extraordinary career" bit. We gave them a drink and gathered somehow that their editors had heard that the poor old gentleman had gone a bit – well! He was out of the room now, and we all smiled, and they said they'd like to be off, if they might. We told them that in the event of death the papers would be notified, and I said I presumed the dictated stuff would be scrapped at once. They laughed and departed.

This remarkable feat of cunning soothed Uncle Mick for a while. Nevertheless, the problem of the date remained. There she lay, and there was no telling at what inconvenient moment she would take her last breath.

Night and day Eric had to assure him that a horse and gig were permanently harnessed in our stables so that he could carry his bad news through the town at an instant's notice – as if such a thing was possible or could be tolerated. But Uncle Mick believed him and the certainty helped. Night and day I swore that I would be at the ready at the telephone the very moment my aunt died.

And then, as inconveniently as possible, she did die, in the bright early morning of Easter Sunday. The Blue Nun said at five-thirty a.m. that it was now definitely all over.

Eric had been keeping vigil, fully dressed, since midnight. Uncle Mick, hardly waiting to say a *de profundis* with the Blue Nun, was downstairs in a flash, shaking Eric awake and into action. He wanted the horse and trap within three minutes, not less. He wanted me woken instantly in my bed at home, to take up my duties at the telephone.

"But it's half past five on Sunday morning, Uncle. There's nothing we can do at this hour, with the trap or at the telephone!"

"I have all her grieving friends to call on! They must hear the bad news at once, God help them all! And Kitty knows she has to speak to all the newspapers!"

"She can't. They're not there!"

"How do you mean, they're not there? The editors live somewhere, man. Go on – run and tell them all at Boru House, and may they not grieve too much, the poor children – and tell Kitty what she has to do – and bring the trap to me at once, sir!"

Eric did not wake any of us, but he thought he had better harness the pony and trap anyway, and perhaps take the old man to Mass or something, to kill a little time. He was not able to manage much, however, because by six o'clock Uncle was ringing and knocking outside the hall door of our newly-married sister Nance, in a distant suburb, and she and Stephen had to stumble downstairs to hear the news, and the "extraordinary career". Eric managed to avoid calls on other households, on the clever plea that the poor people might be allowed to enjoy their breakfast before the blow fell – but any early citizen on his way to Mass was stopped, and heard all. "She loved you, William, and you loved her," he would insist to bewildered near strangers. So he did his best for her funeral, and the correct announcement was in Monday's press.

On that morning one terrible thing happened. I was in the little sun-filled house, when through the doorway came a man called Staunton, who had for years been a gardener at Shannon View. He was a fine, strong man and a good gardener, but – somewhat to the amusement of us children – he went in great fear of Auntie Mick. I was touched by his calling now, and led him upstairs. The death room was very quiet; flowers and candles, and brilliant daylight forcing itself through the drawn yellow blind. The old lady lay in icy peace in her brown habit, a crucifix between her fingers, and her face smoothed now into total gentleness.

Staunton made the Sign of the Cross, and muttered a Hail Mary. Then he leant on the brass footrail of the bed and stared at her.

"She was an auld barge," he said, very clearly.

Uncle Mick came into the room.

"Staunton, look at her!"

"I'm looking," said Staunton. "She was an auld barge."

Uncle Mick was not listening.

"She loved you, Staunton, and you loved her."

"She was an auld barge."

I got Staunton out of the room and downstairs.

"Good-bye, Miss Kitty. She was an auld barge."

Well, she had a fairly good funeral on Tuesday, attended by many who had disliked, or even detested her in life. Uncle Mick was not entirely dissatisfied with it, considering the awkward day she chose for her death. But he thought poorly of the obituaries.

Aunt Annie came to Limerick for the funeral. She had never liked Auntie Mick, nor was there love lost. But it was her duty to attend any of our funerals and she loved a skip to Limerick.

On the afternoon of her arrival she was sitting in our drawing-room, and we were having great fun telling her about the goings-on of the week, and about "She loved you, Staunton..." etc. She especially enjoyed the "extraordinary career" bit; chanted it over with great pleasure. Then in came Uncle Mick to greet her, poor old man, all tears – and she received the whole thing. It was wonderful to watch her face during the "extraordinary career" recital. She knew all our eyes were on her, and she was terrified to blink. She truly was a good player of comedy.

Aunt Mary died in 1926, in her sixtieth year. For forty years she had lived by one rule and in one enclosed place. I was only an occasional visitant in Limerick after 1920, but I think I did see her, for the last time, during the summer of 1923. My impression then – inattentive perhaps – was that she was as beautiful and swift-footed as ever, even if the beauty had grown more edged – but she seemed in aspect and even in manner to be girl eternal.

Nevertheless the years since we had all been children in the Parlour had brought her many sorrows and disappointments. Such of these as may have arisen within the community she commanded one cannot guess, save that assuredly she had some to meet. But from without the walls her still rebelliously human heart was much assaulted; by true griefs, such as Father's death and, less bearable, the deaths of two of Katty's sons, our brothers Tom and Eric, each having died in almost boyhood, and somehow incongruously, in India. But there had been for her too the lesser woe of our general scattering into the world and in somewhat uneasy circumstances – the end of Boru House and our clockwork visits to the Parlour. We were away in places she knew nothing of, chancing our arms at this and that – and some of us doing none too well for a start. That we were young and in health, and not too badly educated, that we had our wits about us, and desired anyhow to lead our own lives – all of this was of no consolation to her against her worldly dreams for Katty's children. She could pray for us, and pray indeed she did, storming God for our spiritual welfare, of course – that we should stay always good and innocent, God help us, and free from all grievous sin.

But that was not enough. And I believe that had an archangel come down and promised her that that prayer was heard, answered and guaranteed for all our lives, that would not have been enough, by any means.

Aunt Mary wanted for every one of us the worldly success that she had eschewed. This was a weakness in her which indeed sometimes maddened some of us in its expression, which could be fussy and could sound ignoble. But it was perhaps her only weakness; it was simply a fault of human love, and I have been amused often to find more than a dash of it in the letters to her family of Teresa of Avila.

For us in Aunt Mary however, as in her arch-conspirator Aunt Fan, it could become very annoying.

About marriage, for instance. Aunt Mary herself would more likely have gone off with the tinkers or become a circus-rider than enter the married state; but it was her intention that Katty's four daughters should marry well, marry young, and into Catholic bourgeois security – the more security the better.

The first in line for these plans was our beautiful eldest sister May who as Mother's first-born and darling was undoubtedly the chief idol of the two aunts in the convent. May was never short of suitors, never was to be indeed as long as it suited her to have them; but she naturally hated to be pestered about them, and the aunts had their ears somehow to the ground in their holy convent, and seemed to know of every cat that jumped in our social set – let's call it! So there would be tiffs and tears sometimes in the Parlour, May taking off for home with flushed cheeks and angry eyes. And God knows you could not blame her.

I remember – already in Father's time and when May can have been only about twenty there turned up from New Zealand or somewhere some Sir Somebody Something, who took a great idea for her. The aunts heard of this, and got somehow hold of all the facts. He was something in the Government of New Zealand, he had splendid money and emoluments, he had an Irish surname and he was a Roman Catholic. I never saw the paragon, but I gathered that he was more or less an old buffer of a fellow. But the aunts plagued May about him – how they could have done so defeats me, but in these matters of the world they could be silly almost to cruelty sometimes. Anyway they even tackled me about his high merits one day.

"A baronet!" said Fan.

"He's not a baronet. He's only a knight!"

"Well, isn't a knight a baronet?"

"No such thing. Anyhow, what does she want with

a baronet? Can't you leave her alone?"

There was a row with me then, and I expect I went home in tears. One too often did in later days from the Presentation Parlour.

Anyhow, to much more charming and real suitors they never saw May give her hand. Now and then she almost did, but always withdrew for her own good reasons. That there was any kind of reason in such conduct the aunts could never understand. Her indifference to what they called her chances was a lasting frustration and even a grief to them.

Neither my sister Clare nor I was any good to them either in the marriage market – so that was three of Katty's daughters who disappointed them grievously. Only one of us, Nance, happening to make a romantic marriage managed also by chance to console them by bringing to them a bridegroom whom they saw to be without fault. Stephen O'Mara, handsome, original-minded, witty, was not only of a distinguished Limerick family, not only wealthy, not only Roman Catholic, but he was also a patriot and one of those committed in loyal service to their adored Eamon de Valera. So that one marriage at least gave them everything they dreamed – only, above all they had wanted and continued to want exactly such a perfect romance for May.

There were other worldly cares too in Aunt Mary's last years – not only the change in our circumstances and the scattering off of the boys to take their chances, but there were all of Aunt Annie's troubles and struggles too, in widowhood with a shop she could not manage at all, and her young children growing up to hard times. Many cold changes did indeed come over that small group which she so persistently loved, during the last decade of Aunt Mary's life – exactly from Father's death to hers.

Still, she had her centre of consolation, her love of God. She lived a great religious life, she had been a great nun. As Mistress of Novices she had learnt and given unusual spiritual force, and throughout her later life she was a pure influence in holiness and austerity. If novices and nuns sometimes tended to adore her to hysteria she knew without any anxiety and without giving pain how to handle such infatuation. I have watched her humorously controlling *Schwärmerei.* I have also observed her power over men. She liked their company, unless they were real bores, and they, because they were not blind, delighted in her. She could make them laugh, she could make them talk; and in matters of school, or building or repairs or the community's health, or any of that general business that as governor of her house she had to conduct with men, she got her way. She was obeyed, and men found it a pleasure to obey Mother Margaret Mary. Any person still left in her convent or in Limerick who knew her will testify to that.

She died without a fuss. That is to say, she died a very painful death, but almost with her boots on – she made her deathbed days as few as she could, but she was a long time walking about, working and praying, in unmentioned agony. She was the holiest person in our family, and I suppose therefore the best.

Aunt Hickey lived a long time – dying in her ninety-fifth year, I believe – in 1929.

Her last years were sorrowful, but borne very certainly with firmness, and even, I imagine, with her kind of cynicism, and many a slow-curving smile above the splendid, large teeth.

The Revolution of Easter 1916 had thrown Uncle Hickey into the last, greatest and most sustained of his loyalist frenzies. The Dublin he knew lay about in smoking ruins, and he was implacable against the men who had dared the outrage. His anger kept him busy and happy until his son's death. But with that he grew silent, and thereafter, enfeebled, moved gently and amiably enough towards senility. His house and land and all his goods were sold in the same year that his son died. So his life was over. But there were three daughters, well married, about Dublin; so he and his Anne had homes to go to, and grandchildren from whom to take amusement and a sense of renewal. I do not know when he died, but it was long before Aunt Hickey.

I want to stay a while longer with Aunt Annie before I say good-bye to her. There are things I remember of her in her hard times that I would like to set down. I stayed in her house for some months at the beginning of 1920 – I was just down from the university, and slack about setting out for England to chose a job. And she indeed was the last one on earth to encourage such tedious action. I was there again in January-February of 1922. During the 1920 visit the Black-and-Tan war was raging; in '22 Ireland was in that painful period of uneasiness between the Treaty with Britain and the outbreak of civil war.

During my Black-and-Tan visit Fermoy was under Curfew Law, and many of the young men the MacCarthys knew were away in the hills, in guerilla warfare. My aunt had never hitherto cared for political argument or seemed to take in political ideas. But the existent idea, the Black-and-Tan situation she understood with disgust and confronted with insolent courage.

Normally she was the most foolishly nervous of women; a mouse, a shying horse, a gaggle of geese put her into the silliest frenzies of fear – and as for a clap of thunder! Well, it was sheer hell to be with her in a thunderstorm, which took from her all sanity, all humour, all self-control.

But the Black-and-Tans enlarged these virtues in her, most endearingly. She knew this jumped-up and undisciplined soldiery to be a brutal outrage and a perpetual cause of horror and tragedy, yet she mainly chose to view them as absurd. A great word of hers when she wanted to be really withering was "Pitiful!" So she would look at those dirty foreign boys and men as they loafed about or scrambled into lorries, and lift her brows and say: "Pitiful!"

She would not serve them or have them served, in her now depleted and ramshackle shop.

"I only serve the Fermoy people," she would say coolly.

"I haven't got what you require." I wonder she was not shot for that; but it would have been a daylight action, which was not that soldiery's favourite line.

She detested the curfew, as she had always detested being told that she mustn't do this or must do that. The idea that she could not go to the pictures when it suited her or walk to the chapel after she had closed the shop exasperated her to near boiling point, night after night. So to calm herself down, she used to give curfew parties.

For these guests must enter her house before nine at night and could not leave it until after six. They were a lively idea and enchanted her who was always a creature of the night, but for others they were an ordeal, and she gave too many of them. Her daughters, just home from school, aged nineteen and seventeen, needed their sleep, and I was young too and needed mine; and as for the four or five young guests that she would summon imperiously, they – young bank clerks or lawyers or young business men of the town – however much in calf-love they might imagine themselves to be, with Moira or Jen or me, such exaggerated sociability strained the young emotion, and the poor boys had their work to do next day. (She could not persuade any of her two or three old bachelor admirers to enter into such uncomfortable follies for her sake. "You're mad, Annie – stark mad.")

However, these parties were a part of her answer to the Black-and-Tans, and usually they were fun up to about two or three o'clock, when most of us grew irritable, sick of tea, sick of cutting sandwiches and singing the Edwardian love-songs Aunt Annie adored. Her eldest daughter Moira used to get into great rows over these parties. She, poor child, was at this time valiantly trying to salvage the fortunes of the shop, which she insisted had to be opened at nine every morning, and so – party or no party – she would go to bed at eleven o'clock every night. Aunt Annie disliked any action that was reasonable; especially at night, when fire and lights were on, she despised commonsense. So Moira, tired and greatly worried at this time, always went to bed in sadness – for her mother could be cruel when she did not get her own way.

We used to play bridge by the hour at those parties – Aunt Annie's glorious bridge. "Hearts of oak are our ships..." she'd sing when that was the lead she wanted. Or "When Adam delved and Eve span..."

A young man would jump from his chair.

"Mrs MacCarthy, I refuse to play with you!"

"Really Jim? Aren't you well? Perhaps if you played the piano for yourself then? Would you like a glass of port?"

And he would laugh and resume his seat.

Many is the grand slam we got, Aunt Annie and I, on her conventions.

She loved her daughter Jen to play and sing for her

"Two sad grey eyes..." and "Roses of Picardy" and "I hear you calling me..." And there was a very sentimental one we picked up somewhere which I had always to sing – "Love me for the day of days..."

And then for me especially, and often *da capo*, sitting by the fire, and without accompaniment, she would sing "Boy Blue" – a wonderful, Victorian ballad –

"It's fine to be six years old, lad –
With pence in a money box...
But I am your old Auntie, darling,
And I cannot marry you."

There were some heartrending verses which would have made Freud smile.

In the years I speak of her business affairs were sliding into a small-town petty chaos and decay from which there was to be, of course, no recovery. A great phrase of hers, were she writing to me about any family grief was "My tears blind me." I used to tease her about it, but often, alas, I saw tears blind her over such sentences as "unless we receive a very substantial payment by return of post..." And she went in terror of her bank manger.

At this time her three sons were schoolboys, the eldest about fifteen, the youngest eight or nine – so she had cause for worry. But though she could spend evenings of worrying her heart out, and assuring me through tears that "The Sacred Heart never forsook the widow or the orphan," she could not manage everyday life at all, or bestow order anywhere. This was not her fault. From her cradle she had had everything done for her, she had been free and unaware of all the routine mechanics of living; in her husband's house she had had good servants, and in his shop there were well-trained and sufficient employees. Now, save when her daughters were home from school or later from the jobs they had to take, she had no housekeeper – and she could not keep a house at all herself; and in the shop, which she could keep less, she had one apprentice boy after another, and that was all.

Her generosity was boundless and her hospitality of the most liberal and sweet. Yet her beloved sons grew up in domestic confusion, of course, and under the great strain of her deepening anxieties. Yet she laughed with them, teased them, enchanted them, and made it all but impossible for them ever to get their home work done. They were beautiful blond boys, good-tempered, dreamy and given to "mitching" off to fish or to ramble up the Blackwater Valley when they should have been at school. The Christian Brothers were always coming with complaints to Aunt Annie, which she did her best to take seriously, but the amused and amusing confusion went on – to the disadvantage, naturally, of boys who would have to enter life the hard way. But whatever of that it is certain that no one of them would have changed his mother for any offerable advantage on earth.

She used to hold court charmingly in the shop to many friends – and that was about all she did there. She had one or two old bachelor admirers who liked to visit her there in her dusty little office, or late in the evening to drink tea with her upstairs.

One in especial, as neat and fidgety a man as she was a casual and easy-going woman, seemed unable to resist her society though she must have sometimes got sharply on his tidy nerves. He was prosperous, shrewd, and kind to her – helped her against the bank manager and, I imagine, sometimes forked out some of those urgently demanded "substantial payments", but if the idea of a belated marriage ever crossed his senses, be sure he blew it away at once in panic. He need not have panicked; he would never have been accepted; her sense of the absurd was far too acute. But she enjoyed his fidgety devotion, and even suffered him to read the paper aloud to her some evenings. That, I suspect, was for a secret laugh, because he read absurdly – Parliamentary debates, and County Council rows.

"Loud cheers an' laffcher," he would read, and Aunt Annie was enchanted.

The respectable man might not have been so blandly devoted to her had he known that all through the troubles, Black-and-Tan and Civil War, her house was always a ready refuge for men on the run, and that her elder daughter, acting often as courier for these through the valleys around never went to their hideouts without parcels of chocolate, cigarettes and whiskey from Aunt Annie, who could not at all afford such gifts.

The last vision of her that comes to me is of her standing by her bed in her long smocked night-gown, her curlers all tightly in place and a novel in her left hand, while her right takes sprinkle after sprinkle of holy water from the little font on the wall. A shake and a prayer for everyone – "for dear Fan...for dear May...for dear Clare...for dear Nance and Stephen...for dear Jack." The list was long, and the surroundings fairly damp, I suppose, before she got into bed.

Her last years must have been very lonely, with the children necessarily flown – but I never heard that she made clamours of self-pity. She was a humorist to the end. She died in 1933, happy in the care of her beloved Blue Nun, a life-long friend, Mother Felicita. She had Addison's disease, a complaint of wasting and weariness rather than of pain.

"I'm feeling very happy, Felicita," she said one

sunny afternoon, and a few minutes later she died.

So Fan was left alone; the last of the four Thornhills, the one they thought they would not raise. No sister left at all.

She was in her sixties now, and still had a long way to go; but not, naturally, at a hard pace, or under any pressure, for she was by now the convent pet and its invalid queen; with the years she was to become its doyenne, a golden jubilarian, and the oldest member of the community.

But suddenly in the 1930s she witnessed a revolutionary change in the Presentation rule. From its foundation the order was an absolutely enclosed one. This enclosure within what was now a near-slum combined with hard work in hot and overcrowded classrooms made for much ill-health among the younger nuns, and for some nervous breaks. So the Bishop of Limerick ordained that for one month of the summer vacation the community should withdraw to some house in the country or by the sea, waiving entirely for that one month their rule of cloister.

There was consternation at first in the community room, and some weeping and heart-searching in the cells. Fear entered many of these locked-away breasts. The Bishop ordained however, that no matter their first scruples, all nuns under fifty were put on obedience to go to the seaside house; but he allowed the elders of the community to decide for themselves whether to obey him or to adhere to their original vow.

This permission was of deep relief to Fan who was totally adjusted now, on her own invalid terms, to the rule she had sought to live by, and felt anyhow that without Mary to guide her she could not by any means consider facing such an unimaginable thing as the modern outside world.

The young nuns rallied from their first shock, and

soon found themselves delighted, exhilarated by the prospect of seeing again the sea and fields and roads and houses – all that they had by no means forgotten. A suitable house was engaged at a suitably lonely and wild village on the Atlantic coast, a village where other communities of nuns regularly took their summer holiday. Talk at recreation in the community room was soon all about the astonishing holiday to come, and the journey by private *chars-à-bancs* across County Clare. Some of the young nuns knew County Clare, and talked of passing by Bunratty Castle, and the town of Ennis, and the rolling, green lands about Ennistymon, and where the sea just appeared – at Lahinch they thought they remembered.

Aunt Fan listened to them all with the benevolence which now in age was making her so much a favourite with the younger nuns.

When they began to cut out bathing costumes for themselves – huge affairs from vast rolls of black cloth, she was at first shocked, but then began to take an interest in the strange labour. Then she found that only a very few of the old sisters, two or three very old ones, were going to stay at home. This pained her. Their vows, her vows, after all, had been taken a long time ago – and she had no desire to alter hers, or see the changed, modern world at all. And when one day she discovered Bernardine and Benignus – almost her contemporaries – excitedly cutting out their bathing suits, her astonishment grew very deep indeed.

In her later years Fan had not troubled her confessor over much with her scruples. As a young nun confession had tormented her and she in consequence had tormented various unfortunate chaplains with her doubts and fancies – as well as tormenting her patient sister Mary. Indeed there was a story from her confessional that a weary priest said to

Fan once:

"You'd better talk that over with Sister Margaret Mary." And Aunt Mary had indeed, over the years, trained her to go to confession calmly, and to stop plaguing her confessors about mere nothings.

Now however a scruple took hold, or a temptation, or a fit of plain envy. She began to fret; she prayed very much, to her sister Mary as well as to many saints, that she be guided for the best in this matter of her vow, and that she might do God's will. There can be little doubt that she gave the chaplain a great deal to listen to, and she certainly worried herself into a deepened condition of invalidism.

Well, to cut a long story, the 1st of August came, and my sister Nance with her little son drove to the Presentation Convent in the morning, to see this really historic exodus. And there, ready before all the others, alone and beautifully stowed in comfort in the best seat in the leading *char-à-banc* sat Fan. Smiling like a seraph, irradiating the happiness of a child.

And for the remaining twenty summers of her life, she was a demon of zest for the summer holiday. Though of course she never swam, or made herself a bathing suit. She was content to direct the younger nuns from the rocky shore.

She was very gentle in old age, and though she would never cease from worrying about Katty's children and Annie's, even she had to grow calm before the ups and downs of our fortunes, accept the wilful and foolish things we did, and simply continue to ask God to guide us better henceforward. We all kept in touch with her over the years, we all were very fond of her – and it was fun when one returned to Limerick to go and sit for many hours with her in the same unchanged parlour, and to try to eat the terrific lunch that she would have commanded. And I recall a story against me in relation to one such return-of-the-native visit. It seems that at the date lipstick, already a commonplace in London, had not yet reached Limerick, and I visited Fan in my best suit, and in general I hope suitably groomed. Well, she made no comment – admired my clothes, I imagine, for she always loved to discuss what one wore, and she seemed to find me in satisfactory order in general. There was no distressing personal remark of the kind she was famous for when we were younger, and still could make upon occasion.

But – the minute I left her, she wrote in despair to my sister Nance, with whom I was staying – an exclamatory, *frightened* letter about poor Kitty's painted mouth! And what on earth had come over the child ? What would her darling mother have said ? And what was to be done about it ?

When my first novel came out, *Without My Cloak*, she wanted very much to read it. Nance explained to her that it was not reading for nuns, and that it would only upset and puzzle her. But still she fretted. So my kind sister took a copy, went through it and pinned certain pages together at several points.

"Now, Fan," she said, "if you don't move the pins you ought to be all right."

And Fan did not move the pins, and she was all right.

She never liked Great Britain, and remained a sort of Fenian to the end. But anything that any of her relatives did was more likely than not to be good and right – so when her eldest great niece, Kay O'Brien, was serving with the WRNS towards the end of World War II Fan was inclined to flagwag a bit for the Allies. And sometime after the war she was one day praising Kay very highly to me in the parlour.

She grew dreamy with praise.

In June 1944 Kay had been stationed near Southampton.

So, said Fan to me:

"Do you remember D-Day in the war?"

"Yes, indeed, Fan. I remember D-Day."

"Well, do you know, darling – on D-Day Kay did the signalling."

In 1948 Fan celebrated her eightieth birthday and her sixtieth year as a nun, her golden jubilee. Thereafter, benignly and even wittily, she did in an unofficial sense more or less rule the Presentation Convent; and in many letters, while the strong handwriting grew feeble, she kept her fond sway over the family. She had always in my memory been large, and now in her uncountable shawls and veils grew larger, larger and very handsome, her smooth face white, her nose most shapely and straight, her pale blue eyes shining tranquilly through gold-rimmed glasses. She grew, as I have said, to be very like Pope John XXIII.

She died slowly and peacefully, when she was eighty-five, in 1953. In the odour of sanctity indeed, and very much mourned by a community of nuns who had grown to venerate as well as love her.

So there they pass, my aunts. No one but I will care about their "short and simple annals". Yet it has rested me to set them down, and to try to find in their modest lives the essence of them. That I have not done. They elude me yet – they in their outward similarities of tradition, education and faith; in their agreement in bigotry, prudery and innocence; in their shared loves and anxieties and their half-concealed antipathies. In the relative simplicity of their obscure lives they were close to each other, all five; in the intricacies of their feelings they were much divided, and often estranged. And for all my searching back, for all my will to reach them, I have not found the very heart of any one of them. So now I can only say good-bye to them, ask them to forgive my impertinent affection, my vulgar probing, and wish that they rest forever in peace.

Also by Poolbeg

The Tallystick

By

Bryan MacMahon

In the treasury of the modern Irish short story, Bryan MacMahon is one of the very few remaining chroniclers of an Ireland that is fast fading, if indeed it has not already disappeared. He is steeped in rural tradition and small-town Irish life of the first half of the century. His previous collection reflected his mastery over such material, and the stories in this collection are a welcome confirmation of the mastery. That, however, is not his only strength. Outstanding among his other accomplishments is his wide knowledge of so many other, often arcane disciplines—history, archaeology, hobbies, meteorology, etc.—so that one is reminded of Goldsmith's couplet,

'And still they gazed, and still the wonder grew
That one small head could carry all he knew.'

'His stories, told in such crystalline prose, reveal the bottomless depths of the human heart.'

Irish Press